For anyone interested in hik̇ [...]ore
about what to expect on the [...] ııng
style, Danny Bernstein shares what she learned on her cross-state journey.
When she saw something intriguing, she interviewed locals and read widely
so she could understand it more fully. In this book, she shares her insights
and knowledge so that other North Carolina travelers can understand and
appreciate our beautiful state even more.

Kate Dixon
Executive Director, Friends of the Mountains-to-Sea Trail

———•◆•———

Remindful of Bill Bryson's *A Walk in the Woods: Rediscovering America on the
Appalachian Trail*, Danny Bernstein's *The Mountains-to-Sea Trail* also isn't a
trail guide per se. It's a travel book. Whereas Bryson could be dour (not to
say grumpy) at times, the reader senses right away there's no other place
Bernstein would rather have been than on that trail and adjacent byways,
recording the incidents and personalities, anecdotes and reflections,
landscapes and legends, and natural history observations brought to life in
her book. This will find its place among the front ranks of books depicting
outdoor life and travel in North Carolina.

George Ellison
Author of *Blue Ridge Nature Journal*

———•◆•———

Danny Bernstein not only delivers a fascinating description of the trail
from the mountains to the sea, but she also provides compelling historical
information associated with her route, a firsthand account about the people
and places encountered and a feel for the dramatic and varied landscape
across North Carolina. Finally, she shares through her eyes and words the
beauty and interesting qualities of the land and the wonders of the varied
flora and fauna she observed, making her world come alive for the reader.
More than an excellent travelogue, this book offers much useful information
for anyone contemplating a walk on the MST. Danny's book is compelling
and destined to become a classic.

William A. Hart Jr.
Author of *3000 Miles in the Great Smokies*

# *The* MOUNTAINS-TO-SEA Trail Across North Carolina

Walking a Thousand Miles through
Wildness, Culture and History

DANNY BERNSTEIN

natural

HISTORY
PRESS

# North Carolina's Mountains-to-Sea Trail

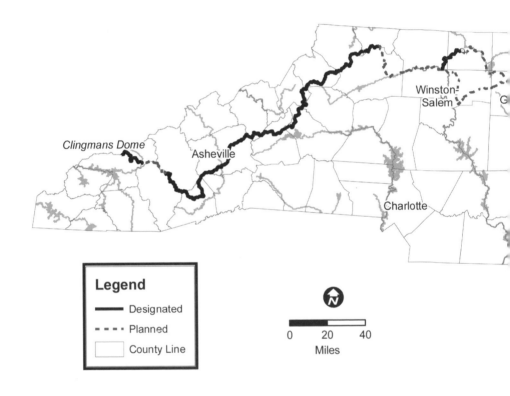

Map of the MST route. *Courtesy of John Amoroso, North Carolina Division of Parks and Recreation.*

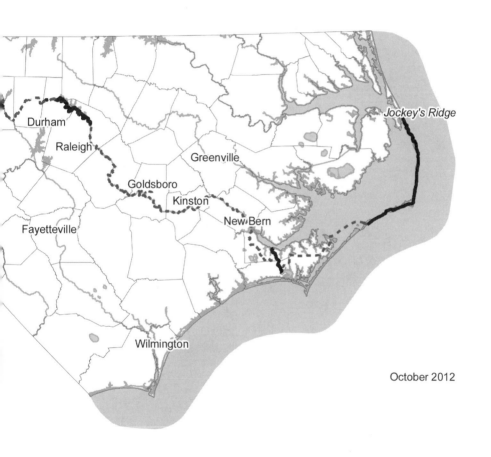

Durham
Raleigh
Greenville
Goldsboro
Kinston
New Bern
Fayetteville
Wilmington

*Jockey's Ridge*

October 2012

Published by Natural History Press
A Division of The History Press
Charleston, SC 29403
www.historypress.net

Copyright © 2013 by Danny Bernstein
All rights reserved

Unless otherwise noted, all images appear courtesy of the author.

First published 2013

Manufactured in the United States

ISBN 978.1.60949.720.0

Library of Congress CIP data applied for.

*Notice*: The information in this book is true and complete to the best of our knowledge. It is offered without guarantee on the part of the author or The History Press. The author and The History Press disclaim all liability in connection with the use of this book.

All rights reserved. No part of this book may be reproduced or transmitted in any form whatsoever without prior written permission from the publisher except in the case of brief quotations embodied in critical articles and reviews.

*To Lenny,*
*who understands that encouragement and support are helpful*
*but time and effort are invaluable.*

# Contents

# CONTENTS

# Acknowledgements

No one does the MST completely alone. You need help of all kinds to walk the MST and understand what you're seeing. Thank you to:

Sharon McCarthy, my hiking partner, without whom I would not have done this trail.

Kate Dixon, executive director of Friends of the MST, who provided invaluable help by answering questions, connecting me with other Friends members and reading and commenting on my manuscript.

Those who walked with me, including Hannah Bernstein, Lenny Bernstein, Neil Bernstein, Kate Dixon, Don Gardner, Joe Hicks, Carolyn Hoopes, John Jaskolka, Janet Martin, Terry Smith, "B" Townes, Dan Wilkinson and Jay Young.

Many others provided important information about the trail. Jeff Brewer patiently answered all my questions about Falls Lake. Brantley and Eugenia Briley offered wonderful hospitality and took me to a cotton farm. Emily Grogan filled me in on the history of the Sauratown Trail. Janet Steddum, author of *The Battle for Falls Lake*, walked me around the old Falls Community to explain her research. Matt Windsor, superintendent of Pilot Mountain State Park, shared the history of the park.

The MST would not exist without dedicated trail builders and maintainers across the state. Thank you to them all.

Thank you to Zoe Rhine and Ann Wright, librarians at the North Carolina Collection of the Pack Memorial Library in Asheville, who always seemed to be able to find the information I needed.

# ACKNOWLEDGEMENTS

Thank you to Adam Ferrell, publishing director, and his staff who guided me through the publishing process with patience and kindness. Thank you also to Darcy Mahan, Katie Parry and Magan Thomas for the editing, production, marketing and dissemination of this book. The History Press is a pleasure to work with.

And thank you to Lenny, my husband, who encouraged me to walk the Mountains-to-Sea Trail, hiked some of the trail with me, read numerous drafts of this book, helped me choose the photographs and was always my head cheerleader.

Introduction

# Walking the Mountains-to-Sea Trail

I decided to walk the Mountains-to-Sea Trail (MST) across North Carolina to really see my state. I've hiked all over the Southern Appalachians for over a decade and feel I know my patch of ground. But what about the rest of the state, beyond large cities with their shopping centers? The MST stretches for one thousand miles across a diverse landscape connecting the mountains to the Atlantic Ocean. It seemed the perfect way for me to understand North Carolina wildness, culture and history.

I've been hiking since my early twenties—and that's a long time ago. I came to the MST after completing many other hiking challenges, including the Appalachian Trail. I've hiked all the trails in Great Smoky Mountains National Park, the New Hampshire and the New England four-thousand-footers and the South Beyond 6000, the forty mountains higher than six thousand feet in the Southeast. However, with the MST, I'm ahead of the hiking crowd. I'm the twenty-first person to walk the whole trail.

The MST starts in the mountains of Western North Carolina on Clingmans Dome, the highest point in Great Smoky Mountains National Park, where you can look over layers and layers of mountains. The trail weaves in and out of the Blue Ridge Parkway through two national forests and eventually to Stone Mountain State Park. In the Piedmont, the MST traverses small towns, greenways and state parks to the outskirts of Durham and Raleigh. It then follows back roads through the Coastal Plains, passing cotton and tobacco fields, roadside cemeteries and churches before entering the city of New Bern. Croatan National Forest is a fascinating world of swamps, bald cypress, snakes, insects and miles of boardwalk. More road walking until the trail reaches the Outer Banks on the beaches of Cape Hatteras National Seashore. The MST ends on the sand dunes of Jockey's Ridge State Park in Nags Head. However, this doesn't mean that the trail is a downhill slide from west to east.

If you travel from Clingmans Dome in the Smokies in a straight line to Jockey's Ridge in the Outer Banks, it's about 525 miles. U.S. 64 is the classic back road across the state from Murphy to Manteo, but that's a driving and bike route. Here we're walking.

The MST meanders to show off the most interesting, scenic, quirky and vibrant in North Carolina. Marked by white circles that dot trees and posts, the trail offers a unique trek through high peaks with outstanding views, lush valleys, rushing streams, farmland and sand dunes. The MST is traditionally divided into four sections: Mountains, Piedmont, Coastal Plains and Outer Banks. The habitat and cultural history of each section changes significantly as you move from west to east. Nothing precludes you from hiking the trail west from the ocean to the mountains. Since the trail is called the Mountains-to-Sea Trail, walking west to east feels more natural to me.

Currently, the MST is about half on footpaths and half on backcountry roads. You also have the option of biking parts of the MST that are now on asphalt until the entire footpath is completed, something that might take decades. I'm not going to live long enough to see it all off the road, so I figured I might as well walk it now.

I've lived in Western North Carolina for over eleven years. As soon as I open my mouth, I get a "You ain't from around here, are you?" Americans are a mobile people, and I'm a North Carolinian now. You don't have to be a North Carolina native or even live in the state to want to walk the MST. Scot Ward from Kentucky has hiked the MST several times and wrote the only current guide to the whole trail, *The Thru-Hikers Manual for the Mountains-to-Sea Trail of North Carolina*. Walt Weber, originally from Maryland, measured and plotted the 140 miles between the Smokies and Mount Mitchell to publish *Trail Profiles and Maps from the Great Smokies to Mountain Mitchell and Beyond*. The MST can already claim its first international completer, William Dolling, who flew over from England several times to walk the trail.

Howard Lee, then secretary of the North Carolina Department of Natural Resources and Community Development, first announced the idea of the MST in 1977. "I don't think we should be locked into the traditional concept of a trail with woods on both sides," Lee said, and I agree. I don't want the whole trail to go through a green tunnel. I like walking the road, meeting people and going into small businesses to buy a cup of coffee or a local newspaper. Sometimes I go in just to let them know about the MST and feel like a trail evangelist. The MST would be a different experience without its people.

The original vision for the MST was not of thru-hiking or even of hiking the whole trail in sections over time. Rather, the MST was going to be the trail in your backyard and close to town. Nevertheless, where there's a line on a map, there'll be hikers who want to walk it all. Anyone can complete the whole trail. You need time, organization and the willingness to be surprised and flexible, but you don't need to be a super athlete. We're not talking about climbing Mount Everest here. Several college students have finished it; so has a seventy-nine-year-old woman from Tennessee.

I invited Sharon McCarthy, a hiking friend from Charlotte, to join me on my MST trek. We plotted, planned and hiked almost all the trail sections together. From the beginning of our adventure, she told me that she wanted to cycle the back roads. I wasn't so sure since I hadn't biked in years, but like in any good partnership, there needs to be compromise. I said I would give it a try. I bought a bike, took a course and rode around the quiet roads of Western North Carolina for practice. After a lot of teeth gnashing, I decided that I would walk the roads. We met up again when the MST got off the asphalt and back on footpath. Looking back on the experience, I'm glad I did it this way. I saw many details that Sharon whizzed by on her bike.

The MST is not the Appalachian Trail!

In a way, the current state of the MST can be compared to the A.T. in the 1950s when so much of the trail was still on private land. That just might explain why only 28 hikers walked the entire MST by the end of 2011. In contrast, 661 hikers finished the A.T. in 2011 alone. But the logistics of hiking the whole MST are much more complicated than those of the A.T. There are no shelters and only a handful of legal places to camp, so backpackers have to be creative in finding a place to stay for the night. Since this is a relatively new trail, still in the design and construction phase in many places, few services have sprung up to cater to MST backpackers: no hostels, shuttle services or all-you-can-eat buffets. Chat rooms, websites, blogs, personal published accounts and mythology about walking the trail, all essential for hikers trying to plan a long-distance hike, are slowly surfacing.

In 1997, Friends of the Mountains-to-Sea Trail, a nonprofit organization, was formed to turn the vision of the MST into a reality. They organize volunteers to build and maintain the trail across the state. They've adopted the same design and construction practices as those used by the Appalachian

Trail. And like the A.T., the MST has to follow the rules of the land it traverses. Another major milestone occurred in 2000 when the MST became part of the North Carolina State Park System.

After writing two guidebooks, I know that the first question from readers will be, "Did you walk it all?" The answer is yes. I drove across two road bridges that I deemed too dangerous to walk on, maybe two miles in all, but I walked every bit of the rest. I blogged about each day on the MST. While writing this book, I went back to hike the new trail sections that became official after I finished the MST.

Writing this book allowed me the privilege of engaging in my favorite activities—hiking, reading and researching, talking to locals and historians and then hiking some more. I didn't set out to write a guidebook or a how-to, though you'll get a good feeling for the route of the MST. Rather, I focused on what I saw on the MST, what fascinated me and what I think will interest you. The MST is a microcosm of almost every environment in the eastern part of the country, except large cities. There are Civil War markers and memorials along the length of the MST, but so much has been written on the Civil War that I decided to leave that history to experts. I don't know of another eastern trail that encompasses Fraser fir trees and pelicans, old textile and gristmills and working cotton and tobacco farms, Revolutionary War sites and two British cemeteries, complete with Union Jacks.

Come on the journey!

# Chapter 1
# Starting in the Mountains

## ROUTE FROM CLINGMANS DOME TO MOUNT MITCHELL—200 MILES

The Mountains-to-Sea Trail starts on Clingmans Dome in Great Smoky Mountains National Park at 6,643 feet, the highest point on the mountains that separate North Carolina and Tennessee. It climbs over ridges and down valleys as it makes its way through the most visited national park in the country. In the summer, dark-eyed juncos flit from tree to tree at high altitude and then move lower down when cold weather sets in. The trail enters the Qualla Boundary, home of the Eastern Band of Cherokee Indians.

The MST continues along the Blue Ridge Parkway for over three hundred miles, connecting parks and forests like pearls on a gold chain. In the mountains, the MST was built using existing trails, old logging railroad grades and carriage roads whenever possible. Here the trail ascends and descends with the contour of the Blue Ridge Parkway and is intimately connected with the road. Casual hikers will talk of "hiking the parkway," but they don't really mean walking on the asphalt. They're referring to the MST. The trail enters and leaves several parks on and off the parkway. East of Asheville, it passes the old walls and stone formation of Rattlesnake Lodge.

Even President and Mrs. Obama walked a mile of the MST when they visited Asheville on a private vacation in 2010. During his weekend trip, the president spent hours on the golf course, but the first couple walked along the trail for an hour with their Secret Service detail. It brought national, though admittedly short-lived, attention to the MST. Hikers were thrilled.

How long you'll want to hike each day is a personal decision. It partly depends on whether you're backpacking or just carrying a daypack. Ten to twelve miles is a comfortable distance for a day hike in the mountains, but the trail comes back to the parkway unevenly so you can't divide the MST in equal sections.

## Clingmans Dome, Highest Point in the Smokies

The first day on the trail starts on Clingmans Dome, the top of Old Smoky. Clingmans Dome Road doesn't open until the first of April because of the likelihood of snow and ice. Even then, park management closes the road whenever it's concerned about the safety of visitors. If the weather is clear, you'll see the characteristic ridges upon ridges of the Southern Appalachians.

Standing on Clingmans Dome gives you an awe-inspiring 360-degree view that captures the heart of the Smokies. "At that location, you realize your hiking possibilities are endless," Great Smoky Mountains National Park superintendent Dale Ditmanson says. "One of the more intriguing hiking options is to embark on a quest for the coast on the Mountains-to-Sea Trail. The trail is the result of a series of dynamic partnerships, which connects the wonderful resources, communities and stories of the people of North Carolina. While exposing hikers to the diversity of the North Carolina landscape, the trail's value will be significant in promoting the outdoors, whether by hiking the trail end to end or just walking a section in a local community."

In good weather, the parking lot is full of tourists. Some visitors are starting hikes, some sit in their cars, but most walk on the outer edge of the parking area, taking pictures of the layers of clouds over the mountains. They're taking in breathless views without becoming breathless. Anyone carrying a backpack will be asked, "Are you doing the Appalachian Trail?"

"Only for a few miles. I'm doing the Mountains-to-Sea Trail through North Carolina. This is where it starts." And you're eager to get going.

You'll pass groups climbing the half-mile paved path to the Clingmans Dome tower. They're exhausted by the steepness and marvel at anyone carrying a backpack. At the intersection with the Appalachian Trail, the

MST gets off the pavement and turns into the woods. But go up the tower to get its famous 360-degree view.

At this altitude, the environment is more like that of Canada than the southeastern United States. It's cold, wet and foggy much of the time. Fraser firs and red spruce, informally known as balsams, dominate the landscape. Clingmans Dome is one of the few areas where Fraser firs grow wild, though they're cultivated on Christmas tree farms at lower altitudes.

On top, the forest looks like a ghost town instead of a green sea of trees. The balsam wooly adelgid, a non-native sucking insect, has attacked Fraser firs, making them appear like giant matchsticks. The insects, which look like white fuzzy cotton candy, were first noticed in the late 1950s on trees perched on mountaintops. Within a few years, most Fraser firs were dead. You can orient yourself with the help of signs set up around the tower. You won't be able to make out the Atlantic Ocean, but on the clearest of days, you might see Mount Mitchell.

Clingmans Dome was named for Thomas Lanier Clingman (1812–1897), a legislator and explorer in the Western North Carolina mountains. Before the Civil War, he served in the North Carolina State House and Senate and then moved on to the United States House and Senate. During the Civil War, he was a brigadier general in the Confederate army. Clingman is always shown with a full beard, wearing a bow tie on a white shirt. He was recognized as the first great booster and a one-man chamber of commerce for Western North Carolina. Clingman explored the mountains in the Mount Mitchell area and argued with Elisha Mitchell over who had first climbed the highest peak.

After Mitchell died in 1857, Clingman led a scientific exploration to the Smokies from Waynesville. The group of six men included Arnold Henry Guyot, a Swiss geographer who mapped the White Mountains of New Hampshire and was now going to do the same in the South. Guyot gained prominence for measuring altitudes accurately, using the best methods of the day. It's difficult to imagine how they managed to go to the top of the mountain; keep in mind that there were no trails or signs at that time. The explorers had to push their way through a tangle of vegetation to what was then called "Smoky Dome." Clingman made the arrangements and hired Robert Collins as a local guide. Collins cut a six-mile path to the top, which allowed Guyot to bring a horse. Guyot named a peak located on the A.T. and MST Mount Collins and renamed the dome after Thomas Clingman. The second-highest mountain in Great Smoky Mountains National Park is named to honor Guyot, but few people hike Mount Guyot since there's no trail to the top.

The Civil War finished Clingman's political career. After the war, he attempted to remain active in the Democratic Party in North Carolina. He promoted the curative powers of tobacco by using it externally as a poultice. He tried his hand at other enterprises, but he ran out of money later on. Clingman owned three hundred acres around the top of Mount Pisgah, which he sold to George Vanderbilt shortly before his death. He never married and died in the state hospital in Morganton. He's buried in Riverside Cemetery in Asheville.

But where is the apostrophe in "Clingmans Dome"? Since 1890, the U.S. Board on Geographic Names has been the official arbiter of American place names. This board decided from the very beginning not to use apostrophes. So Clingmans Dome and other place names usually don't use the possessive form.

Some say that cartographers feared that these punctuation marks could be mistaken for topographic features or symbols. Leaving out the apostrophe reduces the amount of printed type on a map. Another reason might be that apostrophes suggest possession or associations not meant to be used within the body of a proper name. The idea is that geographic names belong to all

A local Boy Scout troop placed the Horace Kephart millstone.

of us. Owning a piece of land is not in itself a reason to name it after the former landlord. Owners come and go, but names live on forever. But what about Martha's Vineyard? Well, if the residents make enough of a fuss, the apostrophe will stay.

The trail bobs up and down, through Fraser firs and spruce as it follows the A.T. heading north. It climbs Little Mount Collins and Mount Collins, both with wooded tops. A view spot was cut by the park, but mostly you'll be between two sets of trees. At a trail intersection, the MST leaves the A.T., crosses Clingmans Dome Road and heads down Fork Ridge Trail.

The trail is a nature walk through a tree identification book, as it descends almost three thousand feet. First, you'll walk through fir seedlings and red spruce. At five thousand feet, the balsams have mostly disappeared and you've entered an area of mountain ash and, farther down, hemlocks. You can hear Deep Creek as you enter a cove. Because of the temperature inversion, it might be colder at this low altitude than higher up the mountain. Deep Creek Trail follows the creek on uneven, slippery rocks. It crosses several feeder streams and a larger tributary. You're in a classic hollow lined with huge hemlocks and rhododendrons. Finally, Campsite #57, a comfortable place for the night. Before taking off your wet boots, walk over to a millstone honoring Horace Kephart.

## HORACE KEPHART, LOVER OF THE SMOKIES

Horace Kephart (1862–1931) was a writer and activist who advocated for the creation of Great Smoky Mountains National Park. Kephart has been called the John Muir of the East and the savior of the Smokies. Several of Horace Kephart's books have never been out of print since they were first published in the early 1900s.

Kephart arrived in Western North Carolina in 1904 when he was forty-two. He was born in central Pennsylvania into a Swiss-German family and grew up within the United Brethren Church. He became an academic librarian, first at Yale. He moved to St. Louis with his wife, Laura, and their first child to become director of the St. Louis Mercantile Library, a subscription library.

As his professional responsibilities increased and his family grew to six children, he became obsessed with the outdoors and looked for a "back of beyond." He took trips into the Ozarks, tinkered with guns and read Nessmuk's book on woodcraft, an early work on the outdoors.

Though he was famous and successful, Kephart felt a deep underlying discontent. He spent more time in the woods and less at work. He also drank more while his wife buffered him from their six children. He was forced to resign from his position in 1903 and suffered a nervous breakdown soon after.

Moving to the Southern Appalachians was to be his salvation and rebirth. But where should he go in Appalachia?

Even in 1904, Kephart found that Asheville and Waynesville were too developed and industrial. So he stayed on the train until Dillsboro and settled in Medlin on Hazel Creek near a copper mine. Medlin no longer exists. When the Tennessee Valley Authority created Fontana Dam, it flooded the only road into the area and cut off access to the outside world. Medlin residents had to move. In the Smokies, he found a place where people lived as he imagined his pioneer ancestors did in Pennsylvania, and he studied the residents around him.

In 1906, Kephart published *Camping and Woodcraft*, a compendium of practical, amusing and historical information on how to survive in the woods comfortably and safely. At the time, most recreational campers used professional guides to explore the woods. In his book, Kephart explained how you could do it yourself. *Camping and Woodcraft* was the mainstay of the Boy Scouts for many years, but now it is a book that one reads for pleasure as much as for advice. Later, he moved to a boardinghouse in Bryson City and wrote *Our Southern Highlanders* about the mountain culture, much in the local vernacular.

When Kephart returned to his first mountain home for a visit, he was shocked by the barren land wrecked by loggers. Kephart became one of the most vocal advocates of the establishment of Great Smoky Mountains National Park. He wrote article after article trying to save the land from loggers. Kephart continued to live in Bryson City and used the old Bryson Place, now Campsite #57, as a summer camping spot.

His articles on the Smokies were illustrated with photographs taken by his friend George Masa. In 1931, a peak on the Boulevard Trail that takes you to Mount LeConte was renamed Mount Kephart, an unusual honor for a living person. A few months later, Kephart was killed in a car crash and was buried in Bryson City. When he died, he knew that the Smokies were going to become a national park, but he didn't live long enough to actually see it happen. Like Moses, Kephart could see the Promised Land but didn't get in.

A few months after his death, the local Boy Scouts formed the Horace Kephart Troop and set the millstone marker on Deep Creek.

It reads: "On this spot Horace Kephart—Dean of American Campers and one of the Principal Founders of the Great Smoky Mountains National Park pitched his last permanent camp."

There have always been Kephart scholars and aficionados in Western North Carolina, but thanks to his great-granddaughter Libby Kephart Hargrove, he has recently had a revival. Libby is the keeper of all things Kephart in her large extended family. She found a manuscript for a novel that Horace Kephart wrote a couple of years before his death. Great Smoky Mountains Association has published it as *Smoky Mountain Magic*. She's organized Horace Kephart Days, a weekend of stories, hikes and a memorial service at his grave site.

Kephart's millstone and Campsite #57 are six miles from the nearest trailhead, so this site is not overrun with visitors. You'll probably have the campsite to yourself.

## CHEROKEE: MORE THAN THE CASINO

The MST drops down to Mingus Mill, the official end of the trail in Great Smoky Mountains National Park. A day in Cherokee might seem premature after only a couple of days on the trail, but visiting the home of the Eastern Band of Cherokee Indians is a fascinating part of your walk through North Carolina. Find an inexpensive motel and spend a day in Cherokee.

The town of Cherokee, the center of the Qualla Boundary, is in a bowl between Soco Gap and the Smokies. It actively courts tourists. Sculptured bears painted with Indian themes stand on every downtown corner. Like many other Indian tribes, the Cherokees have a casino. They've turned Harrah's Cherokee Casino and Resort into the largest single tourist attraction in North Carolina with 3.5 million visitors. The tribe uses its profits well and has improved its community's educational and medical facilities.

The quintessential Cherokee experience is a visit to the casino. The parking area is so large that shuttle buses take guests to the casino, like at an airport. If you have a five-dollar bill ready to change to quarters and like to hear the coins clink as they fall down into the tray, you'll be disappointed. The casino has gone high tech, and you'll need to put money on an electronic card. In the largest part of the casino where smoking is allowed, watching gamblers punch buttons on the slot machines is the best entertainment. The patrons are so intent on their machines that they don't notice anyone looking over their shoulders. The small side room for non-smokers seems a little more sociable. The casino offers several upscale restaurants, which serve alcohol, the only place in town allowed to do so.

Back in town, Grandma's Kitchen offers a huge breakfast buffet with the best or worst of southern fried food: bacon, eggs, sausage, fried apples and white buns. The restaurant would fry coffee if it could, but the grits are great. On a Saturday morning the restaurant is packed. The tribal EMS team takes up a large table.

The Museum of the Cherokee Indian is the obvious first stop. Before visitors are let loose in town, they might want to know the history of its people. The museum explains the Cherokee story with computer-generated images, special effects and many different voices. You'll walk through history from 8000 BC to modern times. Visitors take in more information than they can absorb, but that's true of any good museum. A five-minute movie explains the Cherokee version of the creation of the world with this simple story.

First, the world was all water, and animals wondered what was below. A water beetle ventured to the bottom and brought back soft mud that spread on all sides, creating the land we call Earth. At first, the ground was flat. A Great Buzzard flew over the land. When his wings went up, he created the mountains. When his wings came down, the buzzard formed the valleys. Then a water spider brought fire to the people after everyone else had failed. Cherokees are known as the fire people.

Exhibits start with stone tools and fish traps. The Cherokees built weirs by placing stones in a V-shaped dam along the river. Where stones came together, nets and traps were attached to snare fish. Europeans brought horses and metal items but also diseases. A three-dimensional video shows a medicine man who explains that "for every plant, there's a use, if only we could learn it."

A proclamation of 1763 issued by King George III of Great Britain declared that there would be no more white settlement west of the Appalachian Mountains, but there was no way to enforce it. The Cherokees thought the proclamation protected their land and stood by the king during the American Revolution.

A large exhibit deals with the Trail of Tears, the removal of southeastern Indians to Oklahoma. In 1838, federal authorities forcibly moved the Cherokees. The museum has a huge panorama of removal by wagon, canoe and on foot, much of it in the snow. Thousands died. Cherokees living in North Carolina can trace their lineage back to Oconaluftee Citizen Indians, those who became citizens of the United States. Others hid in the Smoky Mountains, and some managed to come back from Oklahoma.

Across the street, the Qualla Arts Gallery sells exquisite and expensive native art. The town of Cherokee is criticized for having a lot of cheap beads, moccasins and T-shirts made in developing countries. This gallery is the real deal with the high prices to go with them. It offers carvings, masks, cornhusk dolls and baskets from many tribes. A large room in the back shows the history of crafts on the reservation, dating back to the early twentieth century.

On Big Cove Road, find the 120-foot Mingo Falls. The road takes you past the educational complex, a beautiful building for all students in town from kindergarten to twelfth grade. After about five miles, you'll turn into the Mingo Falls parking lot and walk up a long staircase to the falls. After a rain, the water surges down with great force.

Try Paul's Diner for lunch, a traditional Cherokee restaurant that offers rabbit, bison, mountain trout and several hamburger plates. Fried bread is served with everything. The restaurant is not about the food but rather the authentic Cherokee atmosphere, with Indian-themed pictures on the wall and over the fireplace. People sit at a bar in front of a large-screen TV. You can't buy an alcoholic drink in Cherokee except in the casino, but patrons can still watch the big game in comfort. Sit-down chain restaurants have not been attracted to Cherokee because they can't sell beer or wine, which allows Paul's Diner to thrive. A pie case rotates, showing off lavish desserts. You'll love the friendly spirit of the waitresses and other diners. Most are Cherokee.

Tacky kitsch is very visible in Cherokee because, as the merchants will tell you, this is what tourists expect. You can walk past Pan F'r Gold, Native American Dance Shows, Wigwam Motel and many stores selling Indian dolls and toys. Cherokee is not just a tourist attraction but also a real live town with a hospital, supermarket, apartments and a public transit system, which uses large vans. But no Wal-Mart here. This may be the only community that is actively courting Wal-Mart. It's been turned down several times because Wal-Mart doesn't think there's enough business here. The closest Wal-Mart is in Sylva, about fifteen miles away.

Every community needs a bookstore. Talking Leaves is a genuine treasure, but you won't find it accidentally by walking around. This Native American bookstore is in a low building, overshadowed by KFC at the intersection of U.S. 19 and U.S. 441. The shop has books about most native tribes in North America, along with cookbooks, children's literature and every book written by Sherman Alexis, a popular modern Native American author.

## ON THE BLUE RIDGE PARKWAY

The Blue Ridge Parkway is a scenic road that follows the Southern and Central Appalachians for 469 miles. The parkway is considered a north–south road, with Mile 0 at the southern end of Shenandoah National Park in Virginia and Mile 469 at the Oconaluftee entrance of Great Smoky Mountains National Park outside Cherokee. Overlooks, trails and occasional visitor centers offer drivers plenty of chances to get out of their cars. Bollards, short concrete posts, have been placed on the shoulder of the road a mile apart to let you know where you are.

At Scott Creek Overlook, Milepost (MP) 448.4, the MST enters the woods. Carolina Mountain Club (CMC), the largest hiking and trail-maintaining club in Western North Carolina, is responsible for this section. CMC maintains over 140 miles of the MST, currently starting from here to Black Mountain campground past Mount Mitchell. Walt Weber, a club member, wrote *Trail Profiles and Maps from the Great Smokies to Mount Mitchell and Beyond*, which shows the trail profile and where the MST crosses the parkway. Creating a trail in the forest from rocks and trees is a slow process. The club has built a few miles farther west, but for now, the trail continues here.

The trail section is so new and fresh that orange flagging tape is still tied to trees. The white blazes are perfect, and the trail is as wide as a boulevard. There may be a couple of fresh blowdowns if the trail went through a difficult winter and the maintenance crew hasn't gotten there yet. You'll cross a splendid wooden bridge over Woodfin Creek. In spring, bloodroot with its characteristic red stem covers the trail sides. Houses are perched on the mountain overlooking the parkway. Why would anyone want to live up there? How many of these houses are now in foreclosure? What do people do up there, anyway?

The trail drops down to Orchards Overlook and crosses the parkway. The trail is now on the side of the road for a while but still official MST. CMC trail builders are having trouble devising how to get around Waterrock Knob because it is over six thousand feet and very rocky. Maybe they'll decide that the MST will follow the parkway, as it does here for a short section, and not have to go through all the rock around the knob. The trail plunges back into the woods and works itself below the parkway before crossing U.S. 74 at Balsam Gap on an overpass.

## Sylva, a Mountain Trail Town?

Sylva could be a great MST trail town. The Appalachian Trail Conservancy has identified numerous gateway communities along the A.T. that will be advocates for the trail. So why not transfer the concept to the MST? To qualify as a trail town, residents should know about the MST. It might take a long time until Friends of the MST implements trail towns, but it's never too early for hikers to educate business owners about the trail.

A trail town should be small so that residents appreciate that MST hikers are assets that bring in money and publicity to the community. Conversely, hikers get a good feel for the town. Sylva, with less than three square miles and 2,600 people, is the right size. But for most hikers, a trail town is all about services. Traditionally, long-distance hikers look for cheap food and lodging, a laundromat and a post office. Sylva has all of these and more.

Sylva was chartered in 1899 and named the county seat in 1914. The old county courthouse is on a hill overlooking Main Street. When the new Jackson County Justice and Administration Building was completed in 1994, the old building stayed empty until it was restored and reopened as a library

The old county courthouse in Sylva has been turned into the library.

complex in 2011. The building has 107 steps, but if you climb them, you'll find that the steps no longer lead to the entrance. The courthouse lost its majestic entrance in the redesign. Now it's assumed that everyone drives, and the entrance is from the parking lot.

At the top of the stairs, a statue of a Civil War soldier guards what was the front of the building. Every southern town seems to have a Civil War memorial, but in this case, the Civil War was the last major war before the building opened. The Jackson County Museum occupies a room in this complex, but the chances are that you won't catch it open.

Main Street is the classic small-town street with a hair salon, a fly-fishing shop, a bicycle shop, an outfitter and a used bookstore that benefits the library. Massie Furniture Store carries 1950s furniture, the kind that you might remember from your parents' apartment. Jackson General Store sells clothes and dishes and everything else that's supposed to keep you from going to Wal-Mart. Peebles, a one-floor department store that seems to pop up in small towns, sells 1960s-style clothing. The store started in small-town Virginia, though it sold out to Corporate America awhile back.

Up on a hill, City Lights Bookstore is very much alive and stays open until 9:00 p.m. Under the bookstore, a coffee shop and café also serves meals, beer and wine. It's the best place for coffee and goodies.

You'll pass Schulman Street, named after Sol Schulman who owned a clothing store in Sylva for seventy years. His store is now the Penumbra Gallery. Sol Schulman came to Sylva when he was nineteen years old during the Depression. He dressed at least three generations of the town's people. His son, Dave, also had a store here and is now promoting a Heritage Walk through Main Street.

By the railroad tracks, Bridge Park has a great-looking picnic shelter, which would make a good camping spot for long-distance MST walkers. The town would need to install a couple of porta-johns, but that's not going to happen anytime soon. Hikers can stay at Blue Ridge Inn, a privately owned motel with rocking chairs and an outside entrance to each room. Just don't look for rave reviews on TripAdvisor; at this writing; there are *no* reviews.

Mill Street, the backside of Main Street, has two tattoo parlors, several take-out lunch places and a bunch of closed stores. The street also has a brewery and a large dry cleaners—it's the working side of town. Farther on Main Street, Jackson Paper Company makes 100 percent recycled corrugated paper for boxes and discharges only steam. Most of what a long-distance hiker needs is on NC 107 heading south, including Ted's Laundromat and several supermarkets for resupply. All types of fast food are available on the highway. Ryan's and Jade Dragon, all-you-can-eat buffets, will fill up anyone.

The old-fashioned stereotypical view of long-distance hikers is that of recent college graduates consuming as many cheap calories as possible. Not everyone who does a long-distance walk is trying to do it in the most economical way possible. Sometimes hikers want slow food. Lulu's on Main Street is the classic place, but Soul Infusion farther south has, well, soul. They offer over sixty different teas, served properly in a teapot with boiling water. That's the infusion part. The soul is the 1970s funky décor—posters, signs, lei hung on the wall—and friendly people who'll start a conversation from the adjoining table. The restaurant looks to be doing well.

Back in the forest, this section is ablaze with spring wildflowers. It's never certain exactly when the flower show will start or how long it'll last. Early April brings yellow violet, then purple violet, bloodroot, cut-leaf and regular toothworth, hepatica, spring beauties, squirrel corn, trailing arbutus and trout lilies. Later, various types of trillium bloom. The trail parallels the Blue Ridge Parkway and U.S. 74 for a while, and you might see Harrah's Casino in the distance below. The mountains on both sides of the parkway have been cut up by a maze of dirt roads, to prepare the area for high-end houses. Second-home development has taken a dive in Western North Carolina. How many occupied houses will there be? Will the roads stay empty and the forest be permanently scarred? Projects have been failing all along because too many houses are being built.

## Constructing the MST Through the Mountains

It's not easy to turn rock, roots and trees into a trail. Sometimes a new trail follows old roads or horse trails, but the section west of Balsam Gap was constructed from scratch, cut out of a hillside. Where before there was an impenetrable forest, now there's a trail. The work is slow and hard.

Before the trail crew started working here, Carolina Mountain Club negotiated with the State of North Carolina and the Blue Ridge Parkway on the general route for this fifteen-mile segment on parkway land. The state conducted an environmental assessment years ago to see how the trail would affect the land, endangered species and water quality. This first step is often the longest part of the process.

On one workday, the group assembles at Woodfin Cascades Overlook on the Blue Ridge Parkway, MP 446.7. "The purpose today is to have fun," Piet Bodenhorst, the crew leader, says in the parking lot. He starts with a safety lecture. "Stay far enough from others so you don't hit anyone when swinging your tool. Make sure you return the tools where you found them." Loppers, hazel hoes, shovels and fire rakes are strewn everywhere on the ground, in the back of pickups and leaning on cars. The experienced regulars have already selected their tools and task. The rest will be assigned jobs based on where they're needed, but mostly on what they can handle. Everyone is encouraged to participate, from young teenagers to folks over eighty years old. The oldest trail workers have been volunteering regularly for years.

Dwayne Stutzman, the only professional in the bunch, is responsible for determining where the trail goes by flagging the route. Dwayne ensures that the trail stays on parkway land and doesn't veer off onto adjoining private property. He wants to avoid cutting large trees and tries to position the route on the upside of trees where there are fewer roots. He needs to create a gentle slope. Lenny, his helper, acts as his surveyor's stick for the day.

"Now stand up straight and tall, just like your mama taught you," Dwayne says. He positions Lenny next to a tree about one hundred yards in front of him and then, using an inclinometer, measures the angle to the top of Lenny's head. If the angle is 10 percent or less, Dwayne approves it, and they tie a piece of blue surveyor's tape to the tree to mark the route and walk on. If it is more than 10 percent, Dwayne tells Lenny to move left or right, until they get the right slope. By the end of the day, Dwayne has flagged and approved almost a mile of trail.

The section that CMC works on today has already been flagged. The first crew of volunteers bushwhacks up an access route to the head of the flagged section and cuts the undergrowth of vines and low bushes with loppers. The next group takes down trees on the trail. Eventually, all those feet going up and down with chainsaws and loppers create another trail. Alan Frank, a retired dentist, identifies and saws trees to create the first rough cut.

"We try to save trees over six inches in diameter," Alan explains. Trees are not sawed down to the ground because some height is needed for leverage to get the roots out. Alan wears approved gear for certified chainsaw operators: a hard hat, goggles and orange cowboy-style chaps over his pants. To encourage volunteers to work on trails, the U.S. Forest Service offers chainsaw, first aid and CPR courses, all required to use a chainsaw on federal land. Two other men move the downed trees off the trail with their gloved hands or a hazel hoe, which they've wedged in the limb.

Farther on the trail, the next crew pulls large stumps that couldn't be removed by hand with a grip hoist, a small metal winch. A chain is wrapped around the tree trunk, which is only several feet off the ground. The other end of the chain is wrapped around two large trees. A guy cranks up the grip hoist, and the tree roots come out. The idea is like a child who ties one end of a string around his baby tooth and the other end to a door. When the kid slams the door closed, the tooth comes out, hopefully with all its roots.

Piet walks back and forth, helping, encouraging and consulting with each team. As a manufacturing manager in his previous life, he knows how to cajole, joke and work with volunteers. Piet worked with experienced trail crews to learn the principles of trail building. Though the work may look haphazard, the MST follows the same standards as the A.T. The trail should be four feet wide, have an eight-foot clearance and be blazed one thousand feet apart where the route is obvious.

Once the trail is cleared of large trees and roots, it lays exposed so you can examine its condition, like a patient taking off her clothes for a physical. Two teenagers rake leaves and debris off the trail to reveal bare dirt. They came with their parents and were assigned the easiest job to encourage them to come back again. Alex and Brandon and their parents stand out as the youngest in this group of mostly retired folks who go out every week to care for the four hundred miles of trail that CMC maintains in Western North Carolina.

The maintainers in the largest group wield hazel hoes and clippers to get shallow roots and rocks off the trail. You can see results quickly now that the trail is cleared. Carol, a retired teacher, has participated in the trail crew for ten years, and she handles her hazel hoe with a satisfying rhythm. When she puts down the hoe, she uses her loppers to clip roots she just uncovered. Periodically, she smoothes out the trail with the back of the hoe and admires the result.

The benching group has cut a flat vertical line into the side of a slope with hazel hoes. Without a bench, a trail would soon be covered by dirt and soil sliding down the hill. The bench gives a trail feel to the land. Piet shows the bench crew how to create Coweeta dips, a technique that replaces water bars. Water bars were built with a log across the trail and a ditch behind it. "No more water bars, now we talk about water diversions," Piet says. "Hikers like them better than water bars because logs are slippery." A Coweeta dip is a low point between two high spots. If they're built right, Coweeta dips swirl gently up and down, creating an undulating trail that allows a change of pace for the hiker. Shifting the grade or direction of the trail makes it easier to walk.

Hikers tend to walk on the downhill side of a trail so logs and rocks are left on the edge to encourage hikers to move uphill. "We want water to roll off the edge," Piet says. He smoothed the trail with his boots. "The best tool is your feet to finish off the trail. That's why I wear out my boots so quickly." Another group rakes leaves back on the trail to prevent erosion and make the trail look more natural.

The final visible step is painting white MST circle blazes. Howard McDonald wields a paintbrush with the efficiency of the engineer he was for thirty-five years. His paint bucket holds a scraper to file a small part of the bark off the tree, a glue tube with white paint so he can squeeze paint directly on the brush and several glass jars with paint brushes turned upside down. Howard walks west painting circles in one direction and then retraces his steps to paint his way back.

The crew will come back in a year to see how well the trail has stood the test of time and hikers' feet. The work is only finished when individual trail maintainers adopt this section of the MST. Section maintainers take responsibility for about two miles of trail. They walk their piece of trail at least once a season, clipping and weed whacking plants that grow quickly on disturbed land.

Piet says, "Around here, with all this growth, if you leave a trail alone for a couple of years, you won't find it again."

The trail leaves Nantahala National Forest and enters the Middle Prong Wilderness in Pisgah National Forest at Haywood Gap, MP 426.5. Because it's a wilderness area, the blazes have disappeared for the most part, but the trail is clear. The Wilderness Act protects "undeveloped Federal land retaining its primeval character and influence." But the reality is that most places east of the Mississippi are not wild. Mark Woods, who analyzed the Wilderness Act, explains that the land has been "roaded, logged, farmed and otherwise impacted by humans at one time or another." Still, Middle Prong and its companion wilderness, Shining Rock, have no roads going through them. A set of rules was instituted to give the area a feeling of wildness. Besides the lack of blazing, open campfires are not allowed and hiking groups are restricted to ten people.

After the trail crosses NC 215 between the two wilderness areas, a blue-blazed trail comes in from the right. Take the diversion to Devil's Courthouse; it's only about a tenth of a mile. Continue straight up on a gravel trail to reach the lookout on Devil's Courthouse. The massive rock formation at 5,250 feet offers spectacular 360-degree views into four states: North Carolina, South Carolina, Georgia and Tennessee. A metal plaque with compass directions helps visitors identify the mountains in the distance. From the parkway at MP 422.4, tourists can park and walk less than a half mile to the view. Ironically, motorists traveling east will get a better view of the massive rock than hikers coming off the MST.

According to Cherokee legend, a cave deep inside the rock was used as a court to administer justice. The Cherokees called it Judaculla's dancing chambers, and the settlers referred to it as Devil's Courthouse. This rock formation is worth a detour, even if the weather doesn't cooperate and you don't have fabulous views.

## PISGAH FOREST, LAND OF MILK AND HONEY

After forty years of wandering in the wilderness, Moses saw the Promised Land from Mount Pisgah, in present-day Jordan. Legend says that Mount Pisgah in Western North Carolina was named by Reverend James Hall, a Presbyterian minister, who accompanied General Griffith Rutherford's 1776 expedition to eradicate the Cherokee people. Hall was overawed by the rich "land of milk and honey" he saw from the top of the mountain and named it Pisgah, since it overlooked North Carolina's Promised Land.

The trail takes in iconic sights as it wanders from Pisgah National Forest to the parkway and back again. It passes views of Dark Prong Falls and comes down to Skinny Dip Falls and Looking Glass Overlook. For day hikers, the exact location of the MST, Pisgah Forest or Blue Ridge Parkway may be academic. But you can't camp on parkway land, so backpackers need to veer off the trail to find a place to pitch their tents in the national forest.

The ten-mile section between U.S. 276 and NC 151 may be the most popular part of the MST west of Asheville. In spring, grasshoppers jump in a chorus line leading the way. Mountain laurel creates a green tunnel, which bursts into pale pink in June.

The MST climbs steadily toward Pisgah Inn on a perfectly maintained trail. In May, spring flowers are in full bloom at five thousand feet with Vasey's trillium, bluets, blue bead lilies, wild lilies of the valley, lots of wood betony, Michaux's saxifrage, bellworts and several groups of lady slippers. It's like flipping through a flower book. Vast clumps of cinnamon ferns with a red stick in the middle have spread out on the sides.

At five thousand feet, Pisgah Inn has a superb location. The inn offers rooms and meals from March to October. Rumor has it that if you want to stay here in October during leaf season, you had better make a reservation a year in advance. The restaurant looks out on a panorama of surrounding peaks and down into coves. The food is quite good and varied, but diners come for the magnificent view. For MST hikers, Pisgah Inn provides one of the first opportunities to sleep indoors right on the trail. Or you can sit on the porch to eat your packed lunch and enjoy the scenery.

Opposite the inn, Pisgah Campground offers a comfortable place to pitch a tent. There's a tent-only section, so you don't have to camp next to a forty-foot RV, and the campground has even provided large metal food storage bins to keep your dinner away from bears. It's one of the few opportunities to camp on the parkway. In the summer, a small grocery store services the campground.

Close by, the trail to Mount Pisgah starts its steep climb (three miles and 750 feet ascent, round-trip). Mount Pisgah is the first hike newcomers to the area should take. The observation platform can orient you to other features in Pisgah National Forest: west to Cold Mountain and south toward Looking Glass Rock. The transmission tower, used by the local ABC television affiliate, makes it easy to pick Mount Pisgah out of a long lineup of mountain ranges.

## GEORGE VANDERBILT'S BUCK SPRING LODGE

A mile east of the inn, the trail passes an enclosed stone pit, the remains of a root cellar for Buck Spring Lodge. A signboard explains that this cleared area was the site of George Vanderbilt's hunting lodge. Commodore Cornelius Vanderbilt made his wealth in shipping and railroads. George Vanderbilt, one of his many grandsons, built the Biltmore Estate in south Asheville in 1895 and lived the life of a country gentleman. And a true gentleman needed a hunting lodge.

Buck Spring Lodge was staked out on the crest of the ridge with views of Mount Pisgah and Cold Mountain. This was not a one-room hunting cabin in the woods. The site included a main lodge, a stable and a separate kitchen and dining room. The buildings were equipped with running water and indoor plumbing. An army of servants took care of meals and all the needs of the guests.

Vanderbilt built a horse trail from present-day NC 191 close to the Biltmore Estate to Buck Spring Lodge. Called the Shut-In Trail because of the profusion of rhododendrons on both sides, it's now on the MST

Root cellar at Buck Spring Lodge on the Blue Ridge Parkway. *Courtesy of Sharon McCarthy.*

route. Workers came from the other direction. A four-mile wagon road was constructed from the village of Cruso, near Waynesville, to the lodge.

George Vanderbilt died unexpectedly in 1914 after an appendectomy. Edith, his widow, sold almost all the land to the Forest Service to create what is now the Pisgah District of Pisgah National Forest. When Edith remarried, the lodge was closed, fenced in and almost forgotten. But she reopened the lodge again after World War II as a more modest place without the large staff.

When Edith died in 1958, the parkway was in the process of figuring out how to route the road around the Vanderbilt property. The National Park Service was able to acquire the site from the family. Parkway officials felt that they could not maintain the historic buildings adequately, and in 1963, the buildings were removed. Now there's just an exhibit board and three benches for visitors. The board is peeling and becoming hard to read.

Most visitors drive to the site and sit on the benches to admire the view. Behind the sign, you can find some ruins from the lodge. A short trail perpendicular from the MST leads to stone walls and steps enclosed by trees. In Vanderbilt's days, trees were trimmed to reveal a view of Cold Mountain. The trail continues left to the springhouse, the only building still standing.

## ALLEN DE HART, GRANDDADDY OF THE MST

If the MST is North Carolina's Appalachian Trail, Allen de Hart is its Myron Avery. While Benton MacKaye was the dreamer who visualized the A.T., Myron Avery was the dynamo who made the dream come true. Similarly for the MST. Allen has walked the MST, designed much of it, helped build it, wrote about it and started a Friends group to be its champion. Now, in his mid-eighties, Allen is still advising on building new sections of trail.

Allen considers himself a mountain boy. He grew up in Patrick County, Virginia—the closest town is Stuart, birthplace of Jeb Stewart, a Confederate army officer. Allen's uncle was an engineer for the Blue Ridge Parkway. When he was ten years old, Allen was a water boy for the Civilian Conservation Corps on the parkway. "And this is when I also heard about the A.T." The A.T. was completed in 1937.

A couple years later, Allen built a short trail from his house to his school. He calculated that it was faster to walk to school that way than to take the school bus. The trail blended in with its surroundings. Allen remembers it as a piece of art.

Allen's father died before he was born. His grandfather, a businessman, wanted Allen to be a clergyman—Allen's first name is Shepherd—and gave him some land and a car. So in 1943, Allen went to a Bible college after high school. He lasted two weeks. It broke his mother's heart when he came home and told her that he didn't have the calling to be a minister.

"I was concerned that my grandfather would take back the car and everything else he gave me. Ironically, when I went into the army, I was appointed chaplain. They saw that I had read the Bible many times." Allen said.

Allen received a master's degree in history at the University of Virginia and spent a long career as a history professor at Louisburg College, about an hour northeast of Raleigh. He also taught hiking and backpacking courses. When Allen hiked the A.T. in 1978, his students gave him the trail name "Earthdaddy." "My goal was to hike in all the states. I'm missing just four states. I should really go and do this."

"Thirty years ago, I wrote *North Carolina Hiking Trails*, published by Appalachian Mountain Club Books. It was the first book of trails across the state." In those days, the Appalachian Trail Conservancy said that it needed a description of trails connecting to the A.T. in North Carolina. Allen volunteered to write these up. But his publisher thought that the book was too thin, so it suggested adding North Carolina trails in the Smokies and then other trails. The book, now in its fourth edition, contains 1,300 trails.

Allen is an organized man. He's written eleven books and numerous articles. "When I started writing, I wanted to be in a mainstream and understand how publishers worked. I joined writers groups. Growing up on a dairy farm teaches you organization. Cows don't wait. I come from a family of organizers, and I also look for people who are organized."

To write his guidebooks, he measures the trail mileage with a wheel and uses topographic maps for altitude. "Pedometers don't work. Math teaches you that there's only one right answer." He always carried a notebook and created his own trail code to take notes.

"There's lots of public information, but it's not well catalogued. I depend on official information. To work with public agencies, you have to be a diplomat, an inquisitor, a writer with a head."

After the North Carolina Trails Act was passed in 1973, Allen was on the North Carolina Trails Committee for sixteen years. The committee kept hearing from people asking for money for their particular trail. "We needed to think about all trails—hiking, biking, paddling and equestrians. We didn't have money for all of them," Allen recalls.

North Carolina proposed a bicycle route through the state. If a bike route, why not a hiking route? In September 1977, Howard Lee, secretary of the North Carolina Department of Natural Resources and Community Development proposed a Mountains-to-Sea Trail that would serve as a hiking trail across the state. It was an exciting project, but as time went on, Allen felt that the department was not giving the MST the attention it needed. The state wanted hiking clubs to drop the MST name. Allen and others objected.

"So I thought I needed to form my own organization so that the state would have to pay more attention to the trail. Once the MST gets into your system, you can't let it go." He formed Friends of the MST and is still on the board as trail counsel and specialist. He completed his MST hike in 1997 and wrote the first guidebook, *Hiking North Carolina's Mountains-to-Sea Trail*, in 2000.

"Without Allen, there would be no Mountains-to-Sea Trail today," said Kate Dixon, executive director of the Friends of the MST. "Since 1977 when the trail was first proposed, Allen became its fierce advocate. When progress slowed almost to a standstill in the 1990s, he devised a route and set off hiking with a friend to rebuild enthusiasm and show that the dream could be made real. He wrote a guidebook, which allowed others to follow in his footsteps. He founded Friends of the Mountains-to-Sea Trail. Through his passion and knowledge of trail building, he has recruited and trained many trail builders and maintainers who care for more than five hundred miles of trail and extend it forward every day."

"I like a mission and a challenge," Allen said. "I promised Arch Nichols, a longtime trail crew leader in Carolina Mountain Club, that I would finish the segment from Blowing Rock to Stone Mountain." And now this section is completed. "There are many parts of the MST that can be walked on trail now, piece by piece. Soon you'll be able to walk from Clingmans Dome in the Smokies to Stone Mountain State Park, over 330 miles, all on trail in the woods. That will become a national story."

Again, from Kate Dixon, "The MST is the most complex conservation project ever undertaken in North Carolina, and Allen's hard work, vision and passion for the trail are paying off as more and more hikers have a chance to explore North Carolina's extraordinary beauty."

Allen has tremendous drive, as well as physical and mental energy. Besides his books and his work on the MST, Allen started two De Hart Botanical Gardens. One in Virginia has two hundred acres. The second garden is next to his house in Louisburg on eighty-eight acres. Officially called Franklin County Nature Preserve of the De Hart Botanical Gardens, the small private garden is open to the public. He and his wife found several rare plants on their land and decided to create a wildlife sanctuary. The Louisburg garden, with a lake and two loop trails, has been donated to Louisburg College, where he spent a long career. His gardens will live on after he and his wife are gone.

And his next challenge? "When I go to heaven, if there's no MST, I'm going to build one."

## Zipping Around Asheville

From Buck Spring Lodge, the trail goes over Little Pisgah Mountain. Though you'll encounter lots of knobs and bumps, this section is generally easy and well maintained. The eighteen-mile piece, known as the Shut-In Trail, is mostly downhill to the French Broad and NC 191. On the first Saturday in November, hundreds of trail runners assemble to run the Shut-In Trail uphill, starting at the French Broad to the Mount Pisgah parking area. Scott Williams, winner of the Shut-In trail race in 2012, completed the course in two hours and forty minutes. Hikers will take longer.

In early summer, purple spiderworts cover the sides of the trail and Solomon seals have grown to be almost as large as bushes. Later, Turks cap lilies will bloom. The trail comes down to Beaver Dam Gap with a picnic table and garbage cans. On a long-distance hike, garbage cans are useful. In this section, the climb up to Ferrin Knob may be the only challenge. A fire tower is long gone, but a few concrete slabs remain. In this temperate rainforest, everything is lush and green. Close to Asheville, invasive exotics like multiflora rose and honeysuckle abound. Poison ivy, our own nuisance plant, covers the ground.

At Wash Creek Road, under the parkway, you'll enter Bent Creek Experimental Station. The six thousand acres have been an experimental forest since 1925, the oldest experimental forest east of the Mississippi. Before George Vanderbilt bought the land, about one hundred families lived in the Bent Creek area. Landowners burned their parcels every year to clear out the underbrush. Hillsides eroded, and forests filled with deformed trees.

The general mission of Bent Creek is to study hardwood regeneration. Foresters conduct research on logged and abused land. They have facts and figures going back to the Vanderbilt era. Long and large data sets for over one hundred years are their greatest assets. Julia Murphy, interpretive guide for the forest, points out that the U.S. Forest Service hardly ever clear-cuts anymore because of the public outcry. "Yet," Julia contends, "clear-cutting in the Southern Appalachians doesn't bring on the characteristic bare soil and erosion. The forest regenerates itself within a year."

The MST passes by fabric traps, large mesh baskets that catch acorns dropping from oak trees. Every few weeks in the fall, researchers collect, examine and weigh the acorns. These mast production studies measure how much food will be available for bears, squirrels and birds. Mast refers to fruit of forest trees, such as oaks, that provide food for wildlife. The number of acorns is sporadic from year to year, so researchers feel that they need at least ten years of data to understand the variables that affect mast production.

Bent Creek was named for a horseshoe-shaped bend in the creek near the French Broad River. The area attracts mountain bikers from all over the Southeast. Sometimes mountain bikers have a hard time reading maps and signs and staying on bike trails. Mountain biking is not allowed on the MST.

After crossing the French Broad, you can shoot through the twenty miles around Asheville. Here the MST attracts dog walkers, runners and a few hikers and offers urban or commuter hiking. This popular section of the parkway is at low altitude and almost never closes. When you cross over I-26, you can wave at the truck drivers below, and they may wave back. The trail parallels a fence closing off Biltmore Farms, now an upscale housing development. Biltmore Farms was founded in 1897, two years after George

Vanderbilt built Biltmore Estate, his home in Asheville. The enterprise really did produce dairy products until it sold the business in 1985. Then it went into the construction business, building houses and hotels. This land has been lived on. English Ivy crawls on trees and covers the ground.

## Stopping at the
## Blue Ridge Parkway Visitor Center

The Blue Ridge Mountains are older than the Himalayas or the Alps, and the easiest way to see them is on the Blue Ridge Parkway. The road was designed to be a "drive awhile, stop awhile" experience.

The 469-mile Blue Ridge Parkway travels the spine of the Southern Appalachians. Though most visitors drive the parkway, you can walk, cycle or ride a motorcycle. On rare winter days when there's enough snow, you can glide along on cross-country skis.

The parkway was a project designed to employ as many local men as possible to relieve the poverty brought on by the Great Depression. Two national parks were created in Appalachia in the 1930s: Great Smoky Mountains National Park and Shenandoah National Park in Virginia. As a result, logging jobs and property tax money were lost. Building the Blue Ridge Parkway generated wages that immediately circulated into the local economy. But Italian and Spanish immigrant masons worked with local stone to build tunnels, bridges and guard walls. Besides bringing jobs to the Appalachians, the road would also bring in tourist dollars.

The parkway did not rise as a whole from the drawing boards to the scenic road it is today. Rather, the current road is the product of political wrangling and engineering and aesthetic decisions. Drivers wind their way through a carefully designed landscape with many overlooks and can pull off the road to admire and photograph the distant panorama. In many places, trees and bushes were planted to improve land that had been clear-cut and streams muddied by erosion. Bridges and tunnels were built to blend in with the scenery.

No one person is associated with originating the idea of a scenic road through the Appalachians. Senator Harry F. Byrd of Virginia may have suggested the idea to President Roosevelt and provided the political will and energy to move along the proposal. Harold L. Ickes, secretary of the interior under President Roosevelt, implemented the project and decided that the National Park Service would manage the road but not charge a toll.

The States of North Carolina and Virginia bought the land and deeded it to the federal government, which built the road. Stanley Abbott, the first landscape architect on the parkway, selected and enhanced specific view areas. Abbott referred to the road as a necklace with parks and historic sites as its bright jewels. The MST visits almost all these jewels in North Carolina.

Though it's the most visited unit of the National Park Service, the parkway only opened a major year-round visitor center in 2008. Located at MP 384, the visitor center is a short diversion off the MST. The gorgeous building was built to LEED (Leadership in Energy and Environmental Design) standards. The glass and concrete Trombe walls keep heat in long after the sun has set in winter. In the summer, the building overhangs block the sun and prevent the walls from heating up. A green roof with hardy plants helps cool the building and filter out dust and smog.

A twenty-four-minute film, which features scenes shot from helicopters, cars and mountain bikes, puts visitors immediately in the action. The story line follows a father and daughter riding the parkway on motorcycles. For them, it's more than a road trip; it's a way to connect with their heritage. They're on a mission to find the tunnel that her grandfather had worked on.

On the parkway, 168 bridges cut through the mountains. Visitors can build a similar arch bridge out of wood blocks on a table. When done, you can tilt the table and the arch should still hold.

The displays include a mix of the familiar, like the Biltmore Estate built by George Vanderbilt, and the esoteric, such as Carolina Mountain Club's contributions to the protection of mountains and trails. In addition to exhibits on building the parkway, a tableau on recreation shows a picnic setting with plastic dishes and s'mores. Large statues of a hiker and surveyor hang overhead. Yet, the MST is not mentioned in the exhibits. A short connector trail from the visitor center to the MST was built and now is used as part of the Kids in Parks program to "encourage families to stretch their legs on the trail."

Huge photographs are striking. Paul Scott Mowrer (1887–1971), a journalist and poet, is quoted as saying, "There is nothing like walking to get the feel of a country. A fine landscape is like a piece of music; it must be taken at the right tempo. Even a bicycle goes too fast." But the picture on the wall is of a road, not a trail.

The MST passes in front of the Folk Art Center, home to the Southern Highlands Craft Guild, which preserves traditional and contemporary crafts. The modern stone and wood building exhibits the best crafts from over nine hundred craftspeople in nine southeastern states. The guild has embraced contemporary crafts, like glasswork, that are not necessarily part of the Southern Appalachian tradition.

## Rattlesnake Lodge, Summer Home of a Mountain Activist

The MST crosses Bull Gap on Ox Creek Road. Bull Gap may have been named for the last bull elk or the last bull buffalo, depending on the legend you read. After a mile and a half, you'll arrive at Rattlesnake Lodge, the summer home of Asheville physician and CMC founding member Chase Ambler. The family built the house in 1903 and sold it in 1920. It burned to the ground a few years later. Retaining walls and foundations for the swimming pool and barn are still here. The trail passes by the lodge site, a large flat area, stabilized by massive stonework. From the porch of the main house, guests could look down the mountainside into the Swannanoa River basin.

Seven springs are supposed to be on the property. Originally, the springhouse was fully enclosed to keep milk and other foodstuff cool. The remains of the springhouse now have a fallen tree across the top that makes for great climbing. In the spring, daffodil shoots still come up, even after all those years.

On a steep blue-blazed side trail, you'll find the main reservoir, a large stone impoundment with piping that sticks out in the air. But where did the water go? Back down, you can follow the MST and see another reservoir. A series of enclosures funneled water to where it was needed on the property.

It was a good lifestyle for the rich and famous, at least the rich and famous in Asheville. Ambler's wife and children went up to their summer home as soon as school let out, and Dr. Ambler came on weekends. In his pamphlet on Rattlesnake Lodge, A. Chase Ambler Jr., grandson of the patriarch, reminisced about the servants needed to run the house, including a cook and a nanny.

During its first three years, forty-one rattlesnakes were killed on the property, giving the name to the site. Locals throughout the area knew that Dr. Ambler would pay five dollars for any rattler brought to him. Five dollars in those days was about equivalent to one week's wages, so he was offered many snakes, whether or not they were caught on the lodge property.

Ambler owned land from Bull Gap to Lane Pinnacle and, starting in 1912, supervised the building of a horse trail from his property to Mount Mitchell. The trail was supposed to be part of the Crest of the Blue Ridge Highway, a precursor to the Blue Ridge Parkway, but the road was never built. Much of Ambler's trail became part of the MST. At the center of the site, a display board erected by Carolina Mountain Club shows a map, pictures and descriptions of the old lodge and outbuildings.

But Ambler was involved in more than just his own piece of land. He was one of the first advocates for establishing a national park in the Southern Appalachians. In 1899, he helped form the Appalachian National Park Association, though Ambler's future advocacy work veered toward forest conservation. He supported the Weeks Act of 1911, which gave Congress the right to buy land to protect the headwaters of navigable streams. This power created the major national forests in the East.

Today, we remember Chase Ambler in two concrete ways. In the Smokies, Mount Ambler is a knob on the Appalachian Trail on the way to Charlies Bunion. The Curtis Creek tract, the first piece of land bought for Pisgah National Forest, has a large sign dedicating the land to Dr. Chase Ambler.

Ambler must have been indefatigable. He was also chair of the committee that, in 1920, started the Southern Chapter of the Appalachian Mountain Club. The club, established in 1876 in Boston, then had several thousand members and is now considered the East Coast Sierra Club. However, the Southern Chapter lasted only three years. Most of the eight-dollar dues from the Southern Chapter were allocated for trail building in the Northeast. The southern members thought that was unfair and reincorporated as Carolina Mountain Club. Ambler was one of the incorporating members.

At the top of Lane Pinnacle, look down on Beetree Reservoir, Asheville's water supply. Fire pinks, columbines and spiderworts line the trail. So do multiflora roses, an exotic invasive. If Catawba rhododendrons are past their prime, the trail will be covered with purple-pink flowers. The trail heads down to cross Beetree Gap and Craggy Gardens picnic area. This is where you'll normally meet most casual hikers.

The trail runs through an open Civilian Conservation Corps shelter that has been refurbished. A short side trail goes to Craggy Gardens, which explodes with color in mid-June. Here, rhododendron, mountain laurel and flaming azaleas in bloom are jam-packed on top of one another.

A nature trail leads down to the parkway and the Craggy Gardens Visitor Center. The MST turns left and starts a treacherous section. From the nature trail to Greybeard Overlook, the trail is wet, rocky and uneven. Rocks wobble, and roots protrude every which way. Little rivulets cross the trail. You'll walk on a minor road, which leads to Glassmine Overlook MP 361.2 on the parkway.

# Chapter 2
# Continuing Through the Mountains

## ROUTE FROM MOUNT MITCHELL TO STONE MOUNTAIN STATE PARK—200 MILES

The trail goes up to Mount Mitchell, the highest point on the MST and the highest mountain east of the Mississippi, and comes down to Black Mountain Campground and through the ruins of a fish hatchery in the old Mount Mitchell Game Refuge. At the bottom of Bald Knob, the MST joins a small section of the Overmountain Victory Trail.

After crossing the Linville River, the trail climbs out of Linville Gorge toward Table Rock. Linville Gorge is considered one of the most difficult sections, with little water and rugged climbs. Called the Grand Canyon of the East, it's in a wilderness area without signs or blazes. You had better know how to use a map and compass.

Wilson Creek in Pisgah National Forest is not a wilderness area, but it feels like one. The MST climbs on the Tanawha Trail with its rock steps and boardwalks offering wonderful views of the Blue Ridge Parkway's Linn Cove viaduct. Once on top, you'll feel, correctly, that the trail is never going to be as high again.

The MST then enters Price Park, with views of Grandfather Mountain, and crisscrosses Boone Fork. It joins the easy carriage roads of Moses H. Cone Memorial Park and goes through tiny E.B. Jeffress Park. The open meadow views of Doughton Park are breathtaking, but you'll also appreciate the well-manicured trails. The MST keeps coming back to the parkway until Stone Mountain State Park. The road heads north into Virginia while the MST turns away from the mountains to drop into the Piedmont.

# MOUNT MITCHELL, HIGHEST MOUNTAIN IN THE EAST

Three miles from Glassmine Overlook leads to Blackstock Knob and down to NC 128, the road leading to Mount Mitchell. Here the trail comes down almost to the parkway, only to go up again. The gentle section stays shaded for almost four miles, lined with purple-fringed orchids that bloom in June.

The MST leaves Pisgah National Forest and enters Mount Mitchell State Park, the first state park in North Carolina, created in 1915. Governor Craig wanted to protect the land around the mountain from logging. The trail improves greatly, and information signs proliferate. At each intersection, a metal plaque has a map showing your location and explaining the difficulty of the terrain.

The large flat area is the site of the former Camp Alice. Built in 1914, Camp Alice was a tourist stop on the way to Mount Mitchell. A dining tent and several sleeping tents enabled visitors to stay overnight. People came up by railroad to Camp Alice and then climbed to the top of the mountain. When logging was no longer allowed, the railroad carried only visitors, but it was not profitable and it closed down. Later a one-way toll road was built; passenger cars went up in the morning and down in the afternoon. Camp Alice expanded to offer food and lodging until the late 1930s.

Now the trail climbs steeply through a dark spruce-fir forest. Hobbits might peek out of every tree. The trail comes out to a paved side trail where most hikers will head straight for the snack bar. A small museum and bookstore are close by.

If you get to the observation platform by late morning, you'll meet a group of visitors, maybe the first people you've seen today. As the plaque states, Mount Mitchell is the highest point in the East at 6,684 feet. The circular observation platform, reminiscent of the one on Clingmans Dome, was officially opened in the spring of 2009. It requires less maintenance and climbing than the old tower. A map of North Carolina is inset on the walking surface. You have a 360-degree top-of-the-world view, but most of the balsams at this altitude are dead. The trees were attacked by balsam wooly adelgid, the same insect that destroyed the balsams on Clingmans

Mount Mitchell Tower.

Dome. The altitude at Mount Mitchell is only slightly higher than Clingmans Dome, and they share the same environmental problems.

Elisha Mitchell, for whom the mountain was named, is buried below the tower. Mitchell was a Yale graduate who came south to teach at the University of North Carolina in Chapel Hill in 1818. Mitchell started exploring and measuring the Carolina Mountains. In 1835, he showed that the crest of the Black Mountains were the highest eastern mountains. At the time, the accepted belief was that Mount Washington in New Hampshire was the tallest mountain in the East, and many northeastern hikers still believe that. It's on this trip that Mitchell would have climbed the highest peak and calculated its height as 6,672 feet, only 12 feet lower than modern measurements. Not bad for the 1800s.

Later, Mitchell came back to Western North Carolina, climbed various peaks in the Blacks and labeled the present-day Mount Gibbs/Clingmans Peak as the highest one—the mountain now with the transmission towers. At the same time, Congressman Thomas Clingman, a former student, disputed Mitchell's identification and claimed that he had climbed the highest peak first. Clingman and Mitchell wrote letters back and forth. The press published the letters and articles on the dispute, the nineteenth-century equivalent of a Facebook rant.

Mitchell became unsure of what he had climbed years ago and wanted to reconfirm the height of the mountain he thought was the highest. In 1857, he returned to the Blacks. All the references seem to focus on his advancing age; he was sixty-four years old. By now, Mitchell and his party could take a tourist track partway up the mountain and stay in cabins. On his last day, Mitchell went off by himself and was caught in a thunderstorm. He slipped on a rocky ledge above a waterfall and fell to his death. Tom Wilson, a well-known guide in the area, found Mitchell's body several days later. Mitchell's name is now on the highest mountain in the East and the highest on the MST. Clingmans Dome is on the highest point in Tennessee and the highest on the A.T.

From here, you can only go down, but it's not just a downhill slide. The trail stays in the woods most of the time but comes out to several tremendous views. Mica, a silicate mineral that looks like glass, is scattered along the trail.

Black Mountain Campground, on the South Toe River, is a traditional forest campground that attracts families and hikers. It has all the amenities of a drive-in campground, with hard-packed sites, picnic tables and water nearby. The campground bathrooms are badly designed, with two individual buildings, each with a toilet and sink. In the evening, campers can monopolize a toilet for fifteen minutes while brushing and flossing their teeth. The showers are in separate buildings. Why not have men's and women's bathroom blocks? It's a campground, after all. The lights in each little bathroom building stay lit all night, not very energy efficient. For a splurge, you can go back into the park and eat dinner in the restaurant. The menu offers casual park food such as hamburgers, spaghetti, trout, fried chicken and a large selection of pies.

You're at the end of the Carolina Mountain Club maintenance section and have finished *Walt Weber's Trail Profiles and Maps* book. You've left the CMC cocoon and are being thrust into the general MST world. With a copy of Scot Ward's book and keeping up with any changes on the Friends of the MST website and maps, you'll do just fine.

To recap, you've hiked through the Smokies, the Pisgah District, skirted Asheville and moved into the Grandfather District of Pisgah National Forest. Every MST section has good trail maintainers. Friends of the MST has assigned maintenance to local trail enthusiasts, organized into task forces, which are responsible for a section of the trail. But without the details of the ups and downs shown in Walt Weber's book, hikers have to trust the white circles and do a little more preparation.

You're out of the state park and back into Pisgah National Forest. On this stretch, the USDA Forest Service map, *South Toe River, Mount Mitchell & Big Ivy Trail*, is helpful. The difference between national forests and state parks is striking. State parks encourage soft-core adventure. The trails are always well marked and maintained. If there's any confusion or safety concerns, state park officials are quick to put up a warning sign or close the trail. National forests have several missions, and recreation is just one of them. Trails are more difficult to follow and hike. They're much more dependent on volunteers to keep trails open for hiking.

The MST leads out of the campground on a dirt road and up FR-2074. Campers have settled in several primitive campsites, some in tents and others in their trucks. A small village of stone and brick structures, the remnants of Mount Mitchell Fish Hatchery, still stands. Men from the Civilian Conservation Corps built their camp and lived here in the 1930s. Two low structures were once fishponds. The bathroom was in the stone building. Those CCC boys had toilet blocks with all the necessities together in one building. Why couldn't Black Mountain Campgrounds do the same? A stone archway stands on the other side of the road along with the remains of a chimney.

The trail then turns into the woods with beautiful switchbacks. White rosebay rhododendrons and pipsissewa, small white flowers with variegated leaves, bloom here. The trail goes over a tunnel and down to NC 80.

## Up Bald Knob, the Toughest Climb of the MST

From NC 80, the MST plunges into the woods, leaving the Blue Ridge Parkway for a while. The trail climbs up to Woods Mountain and comes down at Woodlawn Park, north of Marion. Allen de Hart wrote that the trail from Woodlawn Park to Kistler Memorial Highway is the hardest section on the MST. From Woodland Park on U.S. 221, the trail goes deep into the forest and doesn't reach another road for 15.4 miles. There's no reasonable way to break up this stretch of trail.

The first few miles in the cool of the morning are on forest roads, which meander through open fields. You'll cross the North Fork of the Catawba River on a long, solid bridge, built in 2005. Before that, MST hikers had to wade through muddy water. After crossing the tracks of the Clinchfield Railroad, the climb to Bald Knob starts. It's relentless. On this ascent, it might be good to practice resting steps, a technique that you save for something this difficult. You need to step and rest, step and rest. The step is so slow that you can breathe normally. Planting your foot on the ground completely before moving the next foot enables the muscles to relax.

The trail to Bald Knob switchbacks to offer several steep and rocky lookouts. Then the trail plunges down only to climb again without switchbacks to Dobson Knob. It's tough, but the trail is so well maintained and blazed that there's never any question of where to go. If you can hike this, thank a trail maintainer—in this case, the Bald Knob Task Force. How do these folks maintain this long stretch of trail? They've made a difficult trail much easier.

The Wilderness Society has named this area of the forest a "Mountain Treasure." The environmental organization is trying to bring attention to places in Pisgah and Nantahala Forests that need protection but are not labeled Wilderness Areas. Theoretically, the Forest Service could decide to put in a road or begin logging here. Most of this Mountain Treasure is in old-growth forest with dense undergrowth and stands of Virginia pine that have never been harvested. The MST gives hikers access to this area for the first time. But no one has to fear that hordes are going to explore this section because it's difficult to find and difficult to hike.

The rest of the section is again on pleasant forest roads, lined with orange-fringed orchids. These flowers are not common, and it's strange to see them on the side of a dirt road. You'll pass a small section of the Overmountain Victory Trail (OVVI). An information plaque explains the significance of the trail. In the mountains, you can find pieces of OVVI at Lake James State Park and on the Appalachian Trail. OVVI seems to pop up in bits all over the Southern Appalachians and beyond.


## Overmountain Victory Trail

The South saw plenty of action during the American Revolution. You can visit Cowpens, Guilford Courthouse, Ninety Six and Kings Mountain, where the Overmountain Men won a decisive victory over the Loyalists.

After the French and Indian War, King George III proclaimed that English settlers could not move west of the Blue Ridge Mountains. The land over the mountains was reserved for Native Americans, but many white settlers ignored the ruling. By 1780, the American Revolution had been going on for six years. The British moved south and assumed that the people here would be more loyal to the British Crown than up North. They then would recruit Loyalists to help the British army battle northern Patriots.

Lieutenant General Charles Earl Cornwallis, commander of the British forces in the South, ordered Major Patrick Ferguson into Western North Carolina to recruit and train Loyalists, or Tories, as they are often called. Ferguson sent a message to the "backwater men," saying, "If you do not stop fighting against the King, I shall march this army over the mountains, hang your leader and destroy your homeland with fire and sword."

The major didn't try to win hearts and minds; he operated by threats. Instead of being cowed by Major Ferguson's threats, the Overmountain Men from North Carolina, Virginia and what is now Tennessee gathered under three commanders at Sycamore Shoals, present-day Elizabethton, Tennessee. They decided to cross the Appalachian Mountains and go after the enemy. They marched for fourteen days, meeting a North Carolina militia coming from Elkin in Surry County. Ferguson and his Loyalists waited for them at Kings Mountain, South Carolina.

The Patriots weren't very organized. One of the leaders said, "If in the woods, shelter yourselves and give them Indian play: advance from tree to tree…and killing and disabling all you can."

That suited the Overmountain Men since they didn't take directions well. Like Indians, they hollered each time they fired a shot. The battle lasted about an hour. Major Ferguson was shot and died on the battlefield. This victory was a turning point in the war. More Carolinians joined the ranks of Patriots, and the strength and loyalty of southerners to the cause of independence from Great Britain could no longer be questioned.

The Overmountain Victory Trail commemorates this march. The western end of the trail starts in Abingdon, Virginia, goes through Elizabethton, Tennessee; over the Appalachian Mountains at Yellow Mountain Gap; down to Cowpens National Battlefield, another major encounter with the Tories; and ends at Kings Mountain National Military Park.


## LINVILLE GORGE, REMOTE AND ROCKY

You walk out of the woods and on Kistler Highway for less than a mile. "Highway" is a misnomer; the dirt road follows the western edge of Linville Gorge. The trail climbs to Pinnacle Overlook, where a wooden platform offers exceptional views of Table Rock, Hawksbill and the Linville River.

The river is a long way down there, and Lake James is spread out below. Shortoff Mountain, your next climb on the other side of Linville River, seems very far away.

You may feel like you're in the depths of Linville Gorge as you approach the river, but the map shows that the MST just skirts the Wilderness Area. How are you going to cross the Linville River? Will the water be too high and cold? Maybe you should have brought a rope, but why? So you and your companions can all go down together? What if you had invited a few more hikers, but who's going to want to cross the river just for fun? Somehow, you'll wade through the sixty-foot-wide river. If it's shallow, you'll have a good time.

The trail climbs out of Linville Gorge and starts the steep trek to Shortoff Mountain. This area burned in the summer of 2007, and flowers are reclaiming the area. White snakeroot, milkweed and yellow goldenrod cover the blackened ground. As you climb, the views of Lake James keep getting better. The town of Morganton lies below. When Lake James disappears, the Black Mountains in the distance loom west across the gorge. At the edge of the escarpment, the trail offers several flat overlooks, framed with table mountain and pitch pines. You'll see the rock formations of Sitting Bear, Table Rock Mountain and Hawksbill. Wiseman's View is the most prominent rock face across the gorge.

After Chimney Gap, the trail is steep, over one thousand feet in two miles. Don't rush through the Chimneys; they're the reward for the tough climb you just finished. The Chimneys are not one rocky spire but a set of jagged columns and crevasses. Stone steps have been cut into the rock. Even in fog or rain, the rock pillars that form the Chimneys are spectacular. In single file, you'll squeeze through two columns of pancake rocks.

The picnic and parking area at Table Rock Mountain doesn't have drinking water. From here, climbers access the Chimneys when they're not closed to protect peregrine falcons. The MST heads up for a short while and then plunges into the woods. If you want to take in one last good view of Linville Gorge and see the Chimneys from a different angle, take the diversion to the summit of Table Mountain—it's less than a half mile. After crossing NC 181, the MST enters Wilson Creek, part of the National Wild and Scenic River System. The area is lush with pines, rhododendrons, mountain laurels and sourwoods. The trail passes a complex set of small waterfalls, crossing Harper Creek several times.

## TANAWHA TRAIL ON GRANDFATHER MOUNTAIN

The 13.5-mile Tanawha Trail starts at Beacon Heights Parking Area, MP 305.2 on the Blue Ridge Parkway. Tanawha, which means a fabulous hawk or eagle, was the original Cherokee name for Grandfather Mountain. The section is marked with a white feather along with the MST circles that you've been following. Most of the classic part of the Tanawha Trail lies on the mountainside paralleling the parkway.

The first third from Beacon Heights to Rough Ridge Parking Area is the most challenging section. The trail goes through jagged boulder-strewn terrain around Rough Ridge, where you can see the Piedmont, Linn Cove Viaduct, Hawksbill Mountain, Table Mountain and Grandmother Mountain. Gray's lily, a rare endemic plant found only in meadows and balds in a few northwestern North Carolina counties, grows on this stretch of trail. The small red-orange petals are delicate and not as flamboyant as the more common Turk's cap lily.

Along with the MST white circle, a white feather is used to blaze the Tanawha Trail.

Climbing through rock on the Tanawha Trail.

The trail goes up a wooden staircase and down again around a huge boulder. It crosses a breezeway and passes the Linn Cove Information Station with a model of the Linn Cove Viaduct and a bookstore. The Linn Cove Viaduct traverses the boulder fields of Grandfather Mountain without cutting into the mountain itself. A viaduct, a bridge over land, was the solution to building a road above four thousand feet without ruining Grandfather Mountain. Years of negotiations with Hugh Morton, then the owner of Grandfather Mountain, on exactly where the road should go made this the last completed section of the Blue Ridge Parkway. The viaduct opened to the driving public in 1987, fifty-two years after parkway construction was first started. The Tanawha Trail was completed in the same year.

Past the Visitor Center, you'll walk on a small wheelchair-accessible section of trail and stand directly underneath the parkway to see its underbelly. Then the trail climbs on rock steps and goes under a granite slab. More rocks, more steps as you ascend, wondering where this is all leading.

If you had to choose the most spectacular piece of the Tanawha Trail, the section to show off to visitors, it would be the Wilson Creek Overlook (MP 303.7) to Rough Ridge Overlook (MP 302.9). The boardwalk protects the fragile mountain-heather ecosystem, which is low and slow growing. The 360-degree views include Grandfather Mountain and the classic S curve of the viaduct. The old man with the big nose is lying down in the classic "Old Man of the Mountain" pose. Because of the low vegetation, the view is unobstructed.

Looking down, the parkway is forever present below as it twists around the mountains. Visitors come up from Rough Ridge Overlook just to admire the view and boardwalks. If you can take your eyes off the outstanding scenery beyond, you'll identify blueberry plants and turkey beard with four-feet-high white stalks. Sand myrtle, a small evergreen plant with tiny white flowers, gives the trail the feel of a northern alpine meadow. In late September and early October, the rocky mountainside turns multiple shades of red. From a high point of over 4,700 feet, you start down. There's plenty of climbing left on the MST, but you'll never be as high again.

The second third of the trail, from Rough Ridge Overlook to Boone Fork Overlook, goes through wooded areas and dense vegetation of rhododendrons and mountain laurels. Trails go off to Grandfather Mountain State Park. If you want to leave the MST to explore, you'll need to fill out a hiking permit, but there's no entrance fee into this section of the park.

The last segment of the Tanawha Trail from Boone Fork Overlook to Julian Price Memorial Park meanders through open forests, meadows and glens. This pastoral section is very different from the rest of the trail. The MST no longer parallels the Blue Ridge Parkway and is quieter. The last couple of miles of the trail pass through stock-grazing areas, fence stiles and early spring wildflowers.

The Tanawha Trail ends in the Julian Price Memorial Park campgrounds. Julian Price, head of the Jefferson Standard Life Insurance Company in Greensboro, bought the land as a recreational area for his company's employees. He died unexpectedly in 1946, and his firm donated the land to the parkway. Besides the campground, the park includes several hiking trails and a lake where you can rent boats.

## MOSES H. CONE MEMORIAL PARK,
### A LEGACY FROM THE DENIM KING

From Julian Price Park, the MST climbs up to Rich Mountain Trail in Moses H. Cone Memorial Park. What a wonderful park! Maybe it's the story behind the self-made man from a Jewish German immigrant family that only the nineteenth century could produce. Maybe he's like the great-grandfather you might imagine but never met. Maybe it's the house, which has been compared to a very modest Biltmore Estate. Probably it's because the twenty-five miles of manicured carriage roads are so easy to walk. Moses H. Cone Memorial Park is not a wild, natural place but an elegant, landscaped estate.

"Do not be stingy, but live according to your position and your finances and be particularly liberal toward the poor, and charitable to the needy." This advice comes from a letter that Herman Cone, Moses's father, received from his much older brother-in-law as he, Herman, prepared to leave Germany for the United States. Moses Cone certainly followed this advice.

Moses Cone was the archetypal first-generation American who made good and used his wealth and influence to help others in his community. His father, Herman Cone, left Germany in 1846 and settled in Jonesboro, Tennessee, to open a dry goods and grocery store. Moses, the oldest of Herman's thirteen children, worked in the family business. The business offered finished clothing, which was unusual at the time since most material was sold for home sewing.

Relocated to Baltimore, he and his younger sibling, Ceasar, shifted to textile production. And this is where they made their real money—manufacturing and selling denim material. The brothers moved their operation to Greensboro, North Carolina, to be close to cheap land and labor and cotton supplies; they became the denim kings.

Having made his money, Moses and his wife, Bertha, wanted to build a country estate to display their hard-earned wealth. Moses Cone bought almost 3,600 acres outside Blowing Rock from local farmers. He promised former landowners that they could stay and work on his estate, considered a fair arrangement at the time. Blowing Rock was a nouveau riche town, attracting many summer residents, some from as far away as Florida, who wanted relief from the heat. No one in the area left as large a legacy as Moses Cone.

Cone hired Orlo Epps, a prominent Greensboro architect, to design Flat Top Manor, Moses and Bertha's summer home. Finished in 1891, the twenty-three-room frame house was one of the earliest and grandest Colonial Revival mansions in the state. The house linked the Cones with American and southern traditions and emphasized the family's identification with America. Though Moses Cone looked up to his social betters such as George Vanderbilt, he didn't want to emulate the Biltmore House in Asheville, which was built like a French chateau.

Today, most of the ground floor of Flat Top Manor houses the Parkway Craft Center, another store operated by the Southern Highland Craft Guild. The center sells top-quality pottery, jewelry, weavings and other works made by the best crafters in Appalachia. A smaller room to the left, once Cone's billiard room, is now a bookstore. His office has been turned into a park office.

Until recently, the ground floor was the only part of the house accessible to the public. But several years ago, the Blue Ridge Parkway opened the second floor for tours in the summer.

"Once you were invited upstairs, you knew you'd made it," interpretive ranger Sandy Adair says. If visitors could tour the rooms by themselves, the second floor would be just a bunch of empty white rooms. However, when Adair gives a tour, the house and the Cone family come alive. She explains that the upstairs is bare because Bertha left all her possessions to her family, friends and workers.

Moses and Bertha's large master bedroom suite has a huge walk-in closet and a private bath with a claw-foot bathtub. The other bedrooms on the second floor were for family and guests. Bertha's unmarried sisters, Sophie and Clementine Lindau, visited for the whole summer to escape the Baltimore heat. The Cones had no children.

The third-floor attic, closed to the public, housed a kitchen and rooms for servants, and children of guests and their nannies. The Cones' own servants lived in the laundry room building, one of many structures torn down by the National Park Service.

Taking a page from George Vanderbilt's estate, Cone wanted his property to be self-sustaining. He consulted noted forester Gifford Pinchot, who had also worked on the Biltmore Estate. Cone planted apple trees and built several barns to sort and process apples. His orchards contained a wide variety of old southern apples; some strains are now rare and should be preserved.

Like all parks on the Blue Ridge Parkway, the trails are well maintained and signposted. Walking here is not a solitary experience. People hike, jog and walk their dogs on leashes. Horseback riding is allowed on most trails. Horse people will point out that Moses and Bertha developed the roads for horses and carriage rides, not for walkers.

Spring brings a wealth of wildflowers, including bloodroot and spring beauties. Later, rhododendrons burst out in bloom. In summer, the sides of the carriage road show off spiderwort, bowman's root, jewel weed, joe-pye weeds, firepinks and larkspur. The park is at four thousand feet, so fall colors come early. In winter, if you're lucky to get enough snow, the carriage roads offer a splendid cross-country ski adventure.

The Cones were Jewish and loved by all in the Blowing Rock community. At his funeral, a Baptist minister slipped a Bible in Moses Cone's coffin, but it looked like he might have been searching for something. That started a rumor that valuables were buried with the body. In 1924, grave robbers disinterred the body. With picks and a sledgehammer, they went through the concrete covering. In the Jewish tradition, the casket was wood instead of steel. Bertha reburied the body and recovered the coffin with concrete. She was so shaken up by this incident that she decided to be cremated. Moses, Bertha and her two sisters are buried in the park, on a side trail off Flat Top Trail.

During his lifetime, Cone was recognized as a great philanthropist; he practically adopted Blowing Rock. He was on the board of the future Appalachian State University and funded the Sandy Flats School, close to his estate. When it was no longer needed as a school, it became Sandy Flats Baptist Church, still active today. Moses Cone died in 1908 when he was only fifty-one, and his widow, Bertha, never remarried.

It's what happened to his wealth and property after Cone's death that created his legacy. Phil Noblitt, retired public affairs officer for the Blue Ridge Parkway, wrote *A Mansion in the Mountains*, a history of the Cones. When Noblitt first saw the park, he was intrigued by the juxtaposition of mountain crafts sold in a palatial home and wondered, "What's the story here?" A history professor at Appalachian State University encouraged him to research the Cones as part of Noblitt's master's degree in public history.

"Moses died without a will, and this was not an accident," Noblitt says. Moses Cone didn't want his widow to inherit all his property, but he wasn't willing to tell her that himself or to decide what other family members would inherit. His siblings created a trust, which eventually funded Moses Cone Health Systems, now a giant healthcare institution centered in Greensboro. Flat Top Estate would also go to Moses Cone Hospital when Bertha died. No one realized that her heirs would wait another thirty-nine years until Bertha's death in 1947. Two years later, the hospital donated the Cone estate to the Blue Ridge Parkway.

Noblitt explained that the National Park Service didn't know what to do with the estate. Up until then, the Blue Ridge Parkway had emphasized the life of remote settlers in their log cabins. After much consideration, the parkway administrators tore down all the outlying buildings on the Cone estate and turned the manor house into the Parkway Craft Center in 1951. The craft store seemed to fit in with the story that the parkway was trying to tell about mountaineers sewing quilts and whittling native wood.

Several writers have called Cone an outsider, but how can that be? He was born in east Tennessee and spent most of his working life in Greensboro. Maybe it's because he was Jewish. Ed Cone, a great-grandnephew who still lives in Greensboro, explains that there have been Jews in the South since the 1600s. And they didn't come from the Northeast.

Moses and Bertha Cone were not the only Cones to leave a large legacy. Moses's two highly educated unmarried sisters, Claribel and Etta Cone, befriended Gertrude Stein, an American writer living in Paris. Stein introduced them to young artists. For decades, the Cone sisters bought art pieces, starting with Picasso and Matisse, before these artists were famous. They even traded comic pages from the Baltimore newspapers for Picasso's early paintings.

When the Cone brothers, who financed their acquisitions, complained that Claribel and Etta were spending too much money on art, the sisters said that someday their collection would be worth more than all the Cone textile mills. The brothers laughed. The sisters left most of their art collection, now valued at $4 billion, to the Baltimore Museum of Art. They also willed a sizeable collection to Weatherspoon Art Gallery at UNC–Greensboro. In contrast, the Cone Mills have closed down and disappeared.

Moses Cone Hospital in Greensboro, Moses H. Cone Memorial Park on the Blue Ridge Parkway and the art collection at UNC–Greensboro— the Cone textile mills may be gone, but Cone's legacy in North Carolina lives on.

## CREST OF THE BLUE RIDGE:
## GRAZING COWS AND THE STORY OF TOM DULA

For years, the Watauga and South Ashe MST trail crews worked on building a new twenty-five-mile section, which starts on the parkway at MP 291.8. Blowing Rock is about two miles MST east of here. Several years ago, a dedication ceremony brought up these facts: "These twenty-five miles involved 150 volunteers who worked 6,700 hours in 730 workdays. This comes to a value of $75,000."

You have to keep remembering that volunteers build this trail, people with full-time jobs, families and other lives. However, on Saturdays, they work on the MST. Many are not hikers; they just like to get out and work with their hands. And after the trail is completed, the same crew maintains what they built.

As soon as you start on this section, you come to a stile, more like a wooden ladder that you have to scale. After a short piece of trail, another similar ladder stops your stride. Is this an obstacle course? A way to discourage mountain bikers? Robert Frost's poem comes to mind:

> *Good fences make good neighbors...*
> *Why do they make good neighbors?*
> *Isn't it where there are cows?*
> *But here there are no cows.*

But cows have been here and left plenty of evidence. The trail works its way into a pasture. It feels like you're walking in England, maybe too much like England. Americans don't encounter cows on a trail very often. A few cows graze here and raise their heads for a moment to acknowledge hikers before going back to their feed. The Blue Ridge Parkway recognized cattle grazing as a historic practice and leases land to farmers to preserve the landscape. But this is still the United States, and hikers can be confident that the parkway is not going to bring in bulls, which you can find in English pastures.

The new trail feels clean and fresh, like moving to a house that was just built. But the recent construction work has not ruined the wildflowers. In mid-summer, jewelweed, Bowman's root, white bee balm and yellow coneflowers fill in all the spaces not taken up by rhododendrons. The trail keeps returning to the parkway and crosses it numerous times. Grandview Overlook at MP 281.4 offers a grand view of the Yadkin Valley. A few houses are off to the right. A small section of the mountains is streaked by a newly cut road, primed for a housing development. Most of the view offers forested mountaintops and the valley below.

The trail passes Jesse Brown's cabin and a second tiny cabin that was used as a bad weather shelter for Cool Spring Baptist Church. A circuit rider didn't come around that often, and when he did, most of his preaching was under a shade tree. Victoria Logue, in her book *Guide to the Blue Ridge Parkway*, explains that the cabin itself was built by Brown prior to 1840 and moved several times.

E.B. Jeffress Park has a small picnic area. A side trail to the Cascades starts a mile loop to the waterfall. Walk down to the upper viewing platform and then the lower one. The water eventually flows to the Yadkin River. The delicate cascade formed by Falls Creek is worth the extra walk.

In the open pasture, the wind can blow right through a body, but it's warm in the woods. The trail comes close to private land and a fancy deer stand.

You'll walk on a back road past Blue Ridge Baptist Church and its cemetery, which might again remind you of walking in England. The Park Vista Motel right on the trail looks very attractive, but it's been closed for a while.

Close to MP 264.4, the MST is on the left side of the parkway, and you may be in danger of walking right past the Lump. Cross the road, go through the Lump Overlook parking lot and climb the grassy bald for great views north of Stone Mountain and Big Pinnacle in Pilot Mountain State Park.

The Lump Overlook explains the story of Tom Dula, made famous by the Kingston Trio, who sang, "Poor boy, you're going to die." The story is true and happened here in Wilkes County. You can go to Wilkesboro and see the jail where Dula was held.

The story of Tom Dula (pronounced Dooley by folks from Wilkes County) has intrigued writers, historians and songwriters practically from its beginning. The bare-bones story goes like this:

Before the Civil War, Tom Dula started an affair with Ann Melton when they were both young teens in Wilkes County. Then Tom was conscripted into the North Carolina Troops. When he came back unharmed in 1865, he resumed his affair with Ann. By then she was married, but her husband ignored her goings-on.

But Tom was a gay young blade, as they might have said back then, who also courted Laura Foster. Later, Laura's body was found in a shallow grave with a stab wound to the chest. Tom Dula and Ann Melton were both charged with the murder and languished in the Wilkes County jail for two years.

Zebulon B. Vance, former governor of North Carolina, took on the case pro bono. He managed to get the trial moved to Statesville in order to ensure an impartial hearing where supposedly Confederate support was stronger. Still Tom was convicted and hanged. Before he died, he wrote out a confession, saying that he acted alone in the murder of Laura Foster, and Ann Melton was freed. By some accounts, Tom also wrote a song about his situation on the way to his execution.

The song was passed down through the generations. In 1938, Watauga County musician Frank Proffitt recorded the ballad. But the Kingston Trio version created a hit around the world and spread the legend.

As the plaque at the overlook states, "During his last days in jail, tradition says he composed his tragic and still popular song in which he confessed stabbing his sweetheart. But the song did not reveal the other woman who may have done the deed."

The song's most famous lines are:

*Hang down your head, Tom Dooley*
*Hang down your head and cry*
*Hang down your head, Tom Dooley*
*Poor boy you're bound to die.*

But why did Zebulon Vance take the case for free? Some say that the Dula and Melton case became a national news item, which was valuable to politicians even back then. John Foster West, author of *The Ballad of Tom Dula*, speculates that Vance took the case because he represented the Conservative Democrats (the Whigs) and the prosecution was Republican (Abraham Lincoln's party). Perhaps Vance was just thinking about his legacy.

At the overlook, there's a break in the fence, the only evidence that you can go up the hill. A narrow path leads to an open pasture, a smaller version of Max Patch on the Appalachian Trail. Climb to the top. You can twirl in the wind and replay the *Sound of Music* scene with Julie Andrews, though you probably won't have the peasant dress. It's not the Alps, but the wedding cake formation in Pilot Mountain State Park, Hanging Rock and Stone Mountain are in the distance. The panorama is amazing.

The break in the fence to climb here isn't obvious, and there's no sign that says that you can climb to the top. The trail could have been a herd path. If you want to encourage the public to get out of their cars and walk, you should give people the information they need to find the trails. The sense of the woods here is different from the peaks west of Asheville. From the perspective of the whole state, we're still in Western North Carolina. However, with open pastures, small roads, churches and a motel right on the parkway, this area is more rural than wild. After the Lump, it's only about three miles to NC 16, but the trail seems to go on forever.

## Kate Dixon, Friends of the MST

You keep hearing that the MST isn't finished. Kate Dixon, executive director of Friends of the MST, talks about the actual trail and the ultimate trail.

"The current trail is done now. You can walk from the Smoky Mountains to the Atlantic Ocean," Kate says. "But the ultimate trail, the one thousand miles all on footpath, doesn't have a completion time."

Kate is the head cheerleader for the MST. "I've put most of my efforts where there isn't a footpath. I know the needs, and I'm excited about the possibilities of the MST."

Kate was born in New Jersey. "That's where I got the love of the land. My father's family lived in a very rural area around Princeton. My mother's family came from around Lancaster, Pennsylvania." As a child, Kate moved around a lot. She graduated from Hamilton College in upstate New York with a degree in philosophy. "The book *Food First: Beyond the Myth of Scarcity* by Frances Moore Lappe, first published in 1981, about the problems of large-scale agriculture on local economies, really moved me.

"My first job was with an organization in Washington that focused on development policy and relations with developing countries, where I learned to be creative with limited resources." She studied watershed management at the University of Arizona in Tucson and came to Raleigh when her husband got a job here.

"I started with Triangle Land Conservancy, where I was the first full-time staff person. When I left, it had twelve people, a large organization in my context." Kate is good at building nonprofits and likes the startup phase of an organization.

"Then I moved to Land for Tomorrow, a coalition of conservation organizations, which lobbies to protect land in North Carolina," Kate continues. "I was looking for people who would get involved in conservation. Friends of the MST was one of the members, and I met Jeff Brewer, then president of FMST. I started with FMST in 2008."

Kate's job is diverse. She explains, "I'm best at building small organizations. I work with all those people who put in so much time with so little money. When I came in, FMST hadn't reached out to land trusts or local government. This job is the perfect mesh of everything I do. I think that the MST is a really exciting project."

Kate doesn't feel that everyone needs to hike the whole trail. "Some of our supporters may never hike the trail or maintain it. They're interested in the vision. And the vision is to be able to walk on trails from the Smoky Mountains to the coast."

Less than five hundred miles of the MST are still on the road. Acquiring land is the biggest hurdle. Then the trail needs to be mapped and constructed. Over one hundred miles of trail have opened up under Kate's watch. That's a sizeable fraction of one thousand miles.

## Doughton Park: Bluffs and Meadows

The trail crisscrosses the Blue Ridge Parkway and lots of small roads. Here, the parkway is not the pristine quiet road that you've gotten used to farther south. Locals use the parkway as a commuter road; they're commuting in a national park. Tourists drive this section to admire the autumn colors, but as a hiker, you're *in* the colors. Red maples and yellowing Fraser magnolias abound. This is not a place to daydream. Hikers have to pay attention to the white circles as the MST changes from trail to back roads to parkway. The MST goes above the parkway and parallels it at many points.

The trail encircles the Northwest Trading Post, a gift shop and snack bar that sits squarely on the parkway. Why the circuitous route? Who knows what local decisions were made to have hikers go around the building? It's a good place for fudge and other snacks, but you don't want to be carrying pottery on the trail. You pass two cemetery gates, including the Sheets Cemetery. Later the Jesse Sheets Cabin, built in 1815, is down a small hill off the parkway.

On NC 18, you're in downtown Laurel Springs, the motorcycle capital of the parkway. The community consists of two motels, two antique shops and a country store. If you plan to stay here overnight, make reservations and check what facilities are open. For example, Freeborne's Eatery and Lodge only serves breakfast seasonally.

The Country Store has a sad selection of chips, beer, cookies and snacks, but you can spend a lot of time in the cavernous antique shop next to Freeborne's. The owner, who calls herself "Blondie," sells original movie posters, including one of Danielle Darrieux, a French movie star whose career spanned eight decades (important only because this author was named after Darrieux). Blondie sells country music records, toys, jewelry and other kitschy paraphernalia. You can search for hours through old stuff. It's a destination for antique seekers, and Blondie seems to be doing quite well.

Freeborne's attracts motorcyclists and anyone else who likes to eat well. Even on a cold autumn weeknight, the dining room is busy. Groups that have come for a weekly get-together take up the long tables. Bar stools are all occupied by singles having dinner, and the waiters are rushed off their feet. A musician sings old country standards. A framed review of the restaurant appeared in *Our State* magazine. The reviewers loved the food and the atmosphere.

The trail goes past Miller's Campground and reaches the commuter part of the parkway. In this section, cars and trucks fly out of side roads without regard for stop signs. The parkway fans out into a small section of four-lane divided highway. Windshield tourists are taking in the sights. Come on, people. Get out of your cars!

At Basin Cove Overlook, MP 244.7, the trail enters Doughton Park. Here, the MST follows Bluff Mountain Trail, a 7.5-mile trail on the ridge. You'll pass evidence of current and historic farming, such as old barbed wire, stiles, water troughs and fresh cow patties. Wooden posts are left over from old property boundaries and grazing land. A short diversion to Alligator Back Overlook leads to a rocky outcropping. The "Alligator Back" refers to the pinstripe formation on the rock, which looks like scaly skin, but you'll have to get close to see the pattern. After a short paved section, the trail climbs toward Bluff Mountain and switchbacks up and high above the parkway through a dark tunnel of rhododendrons and mountain laurel. Friends of the MST built a wooden staircase and elaborate stonework several years ago.

On top, visitors stroll through mountain meadows with wide-open views of Table Rock and Hawksbill in Linville Gorge due south, maybe even Mount Mitchell. It's like reliving your MST past. A mowed path through grasses leads to a lone tree. In the distance, you'll see the back of Bluff Mountain Lodge, sometimes with cows in the field. It's windy up here.

The MST veers away from the lodge and toward the coffee shop. Unfortunately, both the lodge and the coffee shop have been closed for a few years. Like the other lodges on the parkway, private concessionaires manage Bluff Lodge and the coffee shop, and you can assume that it wasn't profitable enough for them to continue. The lodge rooms were dated, without air conditioning and certainly no Wi-Fi, but people who've stayed here felt that it was part of the appeal. Guests sat on the balcony with a fire going and conversed like one big family.

The coffee shop opened in 1949, and a couple of the original waitresses were still working there in 2010, before it closed. They served good southern country food for breakfast and lunch, such as fried chicken, ham and barbecue pork. Their coleslaw was superb. The National Park Service has sent out a "Request for Expression of Interest for Concession Facilities." People who travel the parkway just to eat at the coffee shop are waiting for another concessionaire to reopen the facilities soon.

For the last few years, the parkway has worked to restore the rock walls that line the road around Doughton Park. Stone guard walls have been sinking into the ground since they were installed in the 1930s because of the freeze-thaw cycle. About twenty-eight miles of walls need to be replaced. Sediment protectors, snake-like tubes of wood shavings, were first installed below the road so that sediment doesn't ruin the vegetation. The National Park Service feels that these walls are part of the visual and historic character of the road. Unfortunately, while the work is being done, the parkway was closed here and there. It's only a small closure at any one time, but the average tourist may not be able to figure out exactly what's open and closed. These closures couldn't have helped the bottom line for the previous concessionaires.

The trail goes through the campground and past Brinegar Cabin. In 1876, at age nineteen, Martin Brinegar bought a 125-acre farm. He married sixteen-year-old Caroline two years later. They say that children grow up too fast today, but not too many nineteen-year-old men would have the money or the interest to buy a farm today and prepare for marriage. They stayed married until Martin's death at age sixty-eight.

They raised three children and seemed to live well for the area. They farmed, he made shoes and she gathered and sold medicinal herbs. He must have been an educated man because he was also a justice of the peace and a notary public. After he died, Caroline sold the land to the federal government for the Blue Ridge Parkway in 1935. Though she could have lived out her days in the cabin, she found it too noisy and moved in with one of her daughters. Go down steps below to the springhouse where the water still bubbles out of the ground.

Here the MST is close to Sparta, almost on the Virginia border. Sparta is a small, one–main street town with about two thousand residents. The first piece of the parkway was built here in 1935. You've been following the parkway, with some deviations here and there, since you left the Smokies over three hundred MST miles ago. Here the MST is as far north as it will go and as high. At Devils Garden Overlook (MP 235.7), the MST is at over 3,400 feet. The trail leaves the Blue Ridge Parkway and aims downward.

## Traversing Stone Mountain State Park

The trail goes over a hill and soon enters Stone Mountain State Park at its northwest corner. A sign warns hikers:

*For the next 2.9 miles the MST has been rerouted for your safety.*
*Follow the white blazed trail*
*Stone Mtn Backpacking Parking Lot 5.6 miles*

So the MST was rerouted, but it doesn't say when. Was it this year? A decade ago? You'll turn left as the sign indicates. The MST follows an old road that descends and curves around Scott Ridge. Though you may feel uneasy at the lack of blazes marking the trail, the old road hasn't crossed any other trails. When you pass a cabin in ruins, you'll know that you're following current directions. After more than five miles of downhill, the trail reaches the backcountry parking and registration area. Discussions with locals reveal that the reroute was done at least six years ago. Why is the park still talking about a reroute? The signs are just confusing. An old topographic map shows an aerial tramway.

"When this local man came back from Europe after World War II, he brought back the idea of aerial tramways. He thought he could replicate it here," explains a local hiker.

According to a website, it was supposed to be "the world's longest and highest gondola span." The tram crossed 2,800 feet over the Bullhead Creek chasm, 1,052 feet in the air. People could ride from Mahogany Rock Mountain to Scott Ridge for fifty cents. There was a visitor center, restrooms and gift shop on Scott Ridge. The tourist attraction is gone now, though you can find bits of the tramway if you bushwhack. For MST hikers, the only reminder is the confusing sign.

The trail leads to the Hiker Parking area and starts on the Stone Mountain Loop Trail. The Hutchinson Homestead is a good short diversion off the trail. The Hutchinson family built the house in 1855 and expanded it as their family grew. Four generations lived and worked here. The house is open on weekends during the season, but the farm also has a barn, corncrib, meat and tobacco house and blacksmith shop. The enclosed garden seems to have been overtaken by weeds.

And then the view of Stone Mountain hits you. The Stone Mountain dome rises seven hundred feet from the valley floor. The bare rock is stunning, partly because it's not connected to a mountain range. In geological terms, the rock is a granite pluton, an igneous rock formed beneath the earth's surface by molten lava. Small water runoffs created dark streaks on the rock, and climbers take advantage of cracks in the rock to scale Stone Mountain. The MST doesn't go up to the summit of Stone Mountain, though the trail to the top is well marked.

An elaborate wooden staircase leads to Stone Mountain Falls on Big Sandy Creek. Several flat decks with benches allow hikers to get a better look at the waterfall. On top, water slides over sloped rock into a small pool, gathering momentum for its two-hundred-foot slide. Warning signs are everywhere:

*WARNING!*
*Area contains hazards associated with*
*rocks, steep slopes and cliffs*
*INJURY or DEATH POSSIBLE*
*STAY ON MARKED TRAIL*

These signs don't deter everyone. It's so obvious that visitors shouldn't climb up the waterfall, but almost every year, someone dies trying.

Passing a chimney, the trail goes down to a picnic area and through a pastoral wildlife area to reach the visitor center. Stone Mountain is such a beautiful and diverse park. The views of Stone Mountain and from the top of the mountain are amazing, not to mention the several waterfalls and the historic farm. If only they could take out some of the warning signs.

## WILKES COUNTY'S MOONSHINE PAST

From the start of the MST in the Smokies, the trail frequently passes old forgotten moonshine equipment. But nowhere is the moonshine past celebrated as well as in Stone Mountain State Park and Wilkes County. Here, the heyday of moonshining was from 1920 to the 1960s.

The park visitor center displays moonshine equipment, including a copper pot typical of the small one-person stills that operated in the area. Corn, water and sugar were mixed into a mash and left to ferment. The exhibit explains that a fire was built to cook the mash, and the alcohol in the mash vaporized. In the cooling box, the alcohol vapor condensed back into a liquid. The area offered everything needed for quality moonshine whiskey: swift-flowing creeks of soft water, hardwood trees for fuel and fertile bottomlands to grow corn. Whiskey was much easier to transport than bushels of corn. People living in hollows and on back roads could make a lot more money selling whiskey than selling corn.

Traditionally, moonshine is corn liquor distilled and sold without paying the obligatory taxes. In the United States, alcohol taxes can be traced to Secretary of the Treasury Alexander Hamilton, who needed revenue to finance the Revolutionary War. The tax was repealed but reinstated shortly for the War of 1812. The Civil War brought on more taxes, and this time, the tax on alcohol stayed. The government tax on whiskey is much higher than on beer and wine. And unlike beer and wine, you can't make a drop of moonshine legally for your own consumption without doing the paperwork and paying the taxes.

North Carolina was the first southern state to enact prohibition of alcohol in 1908. But when national Prohibition came into effect in 1920, prices for illegal whiskey jumped because city folks were now also looking for moonshine. Demand for home-produced alcohol was so high that moonshiners would often cut corners, using more sugar than corn for their mash and distilling their concoctions in car radiators, which added toxic levels of lead.

Moonshiners not only had the challenge of making whiskey secretly but also transporting it out of the mountains and evading "revenuers." Stone Mountain State Park is full of these old roads, some now used as trails. According to the former Stone Mountain Park superintendent, moonshiners used back roads through the park to bring their liquor to Sparta, the big town, without hitting a major road. Many young men learned how to drive fast and skillfully while being chased by federal agents. In Wilkes County, Junior Johnson was the most famous of the first generation that turned from moonshine drivers to NASCAR racers.

Moonshine is illegally manufactured liquor, made by the light of the moon. Now, modern distilleries are making moonshine—corn whiskey— legally. Even Junior Johnson has an interest in a legitimate business. Because of its traditionally illegal nature, moonshine was rarely aged, and neither is legal, upscale moonshine. That's one of the major differences between moonshine and bourbon. But can they call it moonshine if they're paying taxes on the alcohol?

After Stone Mountain State Park, you'll start walking back roads. Welcome to the Piedmont!

# Chapter 3

# The Piedmont

The Piedmont is still in the Appalachians, but the terrain is much gentler than in the mountains. The MST undulates, going up a couple hundred feet and back down. Mockingbirds, the signature bird of the area, are everywhere.

The trail leaves Stone Mountain State Park, passing through several tiny hamlets on its way to Elkin, a small town with lots of spirit. This section takes you far north in North Carolina, close to the Virginia border, where several houses display Virginia Tech flags.

At one spot on the road, looking left, you can see Big Pinnacle on Pilot Mountain State Park, Hanging Rock and Fancy Gap in Virginia. The outline of Grandfather Mountain is to the right. The trail goes through Pilot Mountain State Park with its wedding cake top. On the Sauratown Trail, hikers are on private land, the only section of the MST to have this arrangement. The trail climbs to Moore's Wall in Hanging Rock State Park with an outstanding view of the valley and the Winston-Salem skyline below.

A few days on the road take you to Summerfield, the home of a memorial to "Bugler Boy" Gillies, who died in the Revolutionary War. This whole area is full of reminders that the Revolutionary War was fought hard here. The trail parallels Lake Brandt and Lake Townsend in the Greensboro Watershed.

When you walk the road, you'll see that North Carolina is still an agricultural state. Cows, pigs, goats and sheep spread out on large farms.

In Alamance County, the trail passes tiny communities, tobacco barns and dairy farms. North of Burlington, historic Glencoe Mill was a major chapter in the state's textile mill history. A footpath is being built close to the Haw River that will eventually take a few more MST miles off the road. Moving the MST onto trail is a slow process.

Gradually, the area changes from agricultural to pastoral. In Orange County, pampered horses trot to the fence hoping for a handout. The MST enters Eno River State Park in Durham for a welcomed ten miles on a trail past remnants of a pump station. Falls Lake Recreation Area includes sixty miles of the MST. Falls Lake, which cuts across Durham and Raleigh, was built by the U.S. Army Corp of Engineers to control flooding and supply water to the Triangle (Chapel Hill, Raleigh and Durham). In the Raleigh area, Friends of the MST volunteers built the trail, bridges and walkways and now maintain the trail. The trail comes out at Falls of the Neuse and back on the road in suburban Wake Forest.

## Elkin, a Trail Town?

From Stone Mountain State Park, two routes are possible, both on the road at this point. The southern route goes through the town of Elkin in the Yadkin Valley on its way to Pilot Mountain State Park. It won't be easy to move the MST onto a footpath here because there's not a lot of public land. But here and farther east, building greenways may be the answer to creating a footpath off the road. Elkin is working on a greenway that will offer its residents a place to walk or bike safely. The MST could incorporate the greenway into its route. Elkin would also make a good trail town in the Piedmont.

A greenway is a linear open space established along a natural corridor, such as a river, stream or rails-to-trails route, for conservation, recreation and even transportation. This description doesn't sound much different from a trail, but greenways attract walkers who wouldn't ordinarily go into the woods. They can connect parks and historic sites with business and residential areas. People hike, run, bike, rollerblade and walk their dogs. Most of the time, greenways are smoother than trails and have more amenities, like benches and detailed maps.

Elkin, with about four thousand people, is located off I-77 on the way to Stone Mountain State Park. Denise Lyons of the Elkin Valley Trails

Association (EVTA) likes to compare Elkin to Damascus, Virginia, an A.T. trail town. Denise left Elkin for quite a few years and returned to her homeplace. Joe Hicks, another active EVTA member, is also native to the area. He spent over thirty years commuting to his job in Winston-Salem but has always lived here. Both Denise and Joe are Elkin boosters and glad that the MST is going through their town. Unlike the A.T., long-distance hikers walk the MST throughout the year, so they won't be bunching up in town for just a week in the spring—although hikers may not be visiting in the winter because Clingmans Dome Road, which leads to the start of the MST in the Smokies, is closed from December 1 to April 1.

The EVTA group came together in 2010 to fight a common enemy: a company that was going to put a chicken waste incinerator just outside the town. "We fought the company and defeated it by citizen sentiments. Then we turned this negative energy into something positive," Denise said.

It's about seventeen miles from Stone Mountain State Park to Elkin. Bob Hillyer is working to convince landowners to give them an easement so EVTA can build a trail from Stone Mountain to the city limits. A portion of the MST will use the route of the old Elkin and Alleghany Railroad. The group created an alliance with horse riders. According to Joe, the riders said, "We'll help you get the trail in."

The trails group has thought ahead. Camping will be allowed on the trail. They're even talking about installing wooden benches. Now, you don't want to spoil hikers too much. Both the town and Surry County have embraced the idea of a greenway, which will follow Elkin Creek, a tributary of the Yadkin River. Winery tours are very popular here as well, and biking tours through the vineyards will follow.

"We're creating a citizen army to build the trail," Denise says.

Elkin is the eastern start of the Overmountain Victory Trail (OVVI). The trail follows the Patriot route of the 1780 campaign to defeat the Loyalists at Kings Mountain. Abingdon is the western end, and the two branches meet in Morganton. "My great-grandfather, five times over, was with Major Joseph Winston when they marched toward Kings Mountain on the border of North and South Carolina," Joe said. What a genealogical feat to have worked this out!

The MST will come into town following Elkin Creek, on the Elkin and Alleghany Railroad line. The E&A had its first run in 1911. The line was supposed to go sixty miles to Jefferson, but only eighteen miles of track were ever laid. When U.S. 21 was built from Elkin to Sparta, the line became obsolete and was abandoned in 1931. A traditional gristmill and cotton mill were built on Elkin Creek. Later, the Elkin Shoe Factory moved in. Dams were installed in the late 1880s to generate hydropower. The MST goes through an Elkin City park, with jogging trails, a playground, a garden, restrooms and the mustering grounds for OVVI.

What does a town need to be a trail town? In reality, most hikers are not going to do the MST straight through. But the MST will follow Main Street, and they'll find the most important element of a trail town: friendly people. Elkin folks are very warm to visitors. You can't walk two steps on the main street without someone saying hi.

Just off the main street is Harry's Place, on Front Street. They serve great lunches with authentic corn bread. A huge mason jar filled with sweet tea sits on each table. That's the place for lunch. Joe points out Royall's Soda Shoppe with the best hot dog in town and Elk's Pharmacy for necessities. Diana's Books, owned by Cicely McCulloch, is another necessity. She carries the latest books and serves coffee and goodies—a friendly place to have a cuppa and use their Wi-Fi. The post office sits squarely on Main Street.

Elkin's Main Street has many empty buildings but big plans. Toward the end of the street, hikers will find Yadkin Valley General Store, where they can buy trail mix and cold drinks. However, for more choices, you can't beat Combs Butcher, with lots of fresh produce. The city owns Smith-Phillips Lumber, an abandoned building, and hopes to have shops and an office for the Overmountain Trail Association, the Friends group for the OVVI. Elkin even has two laundromats. The trail then leaves town on NC 268.

Laugh if you must, but inexpensive restaurants, a resupply point for food and band-aids and a laundromat are what hikers look for on the trail.


## THROUGH PILOT MOUNTAIN STATE PARK

The MST enters Pilot Mountain State Park on the Corridor Trail, which connects the Yadkin River section of the park with its mountain section. The Corridor Trail has been measured as five and a half miles on the trail, six and a half miles according to the superintendent and six miles in written documentation. Maybe one of those numbers is correct. Though the trail looks flat, the total ascent is over one thousand feet. The MST crosses three roads, none with trail signs, but there are plenty of white circles on the trail.

The Corridor Trail, wide and undulating, is popular with horse riders. The land might look worked-over and abused, but a variety of wildlife and flowers have found their home here. A large black snake crosses a patch of dead leaves. A green "shoelace" snake stays well camouflaged as it slithers through the grass. Several box turtles with yellow hieroglyphics on their shells lumber across the trail.

In the spring, mountain laurel blooms profusely. A flowering strawberry bush is a long way from turning into hearts-a-bustin, its more recognizable form, when the seedpods burst open to reveal bright orange fruit. One lonely pink lady slipper sits high on a mound. At one high spot, you'll have a great view of Big Pinnacle on top of Pilot Mountain State Park.

North Carolina State Parks are very concerned about safety. What if someone needs to be evacuated off the trail? How would visitors be able to tell where they are? So the park put in mileage posts every quarter mile. The idea is that if you're having a problem on the trail and you call in, you'll know your location within a quarter-mile. It's nice to know where you are, but all these posts are a little distracting to hikers.

Big Pinnacle in Pilot Mountain State Park rises 1,400 feet from the surrounding countryside. The Saura Indian tribe, the first people who lived around Pilot Mountain, called it *Jomeokee*, the "great guide." European settlers also depended on Pilot Mountain to direct them on their southern path through the region. Jomeokee and the rocky escarpments of Hanging Rock are all that remain of the ancient Sauratown Mountains. Big Pinnacle and Little Pinnacle are part of a monadnock, a disconnected rock that rises abruptly while the surrounding peaks eroded down into the valley.

Peter Jefferson, father of President Thomas Jefferson, surveyed and mapped the mountain in 1751. The land, first acquired as a land grant, changed hands several times. In 1922, William Spoon, an engineer, and his partner bought the mountain for $4,500. They were only interested in timber on their new property, but a fire soon consumed the best trees. Forced to find other uses for the land, Spoon built a road to the top of Little Pinnacle. The road is still in use today. In 1929, he erected a wooden staircase to Big Pinnacle and opened the mountain to tourists. For fifty cents per car and fifty cents per adult, visitors could drive to the top.

When Spoon felt that managing the mountain was too much for him, he put it up for sale. J.W. Beasley, the next owner, paved the road and put in a swimming pool. But eventually the Beasley family couldn't take care of their park and looked to sell it as well.

At this point, concerned locals feared that the land would be developed. They organized into the Pilot Mountain Preservation and Park Committee and urged the state to buy the property. Almost twelve thousand supporters throughout North Carolina donated to purchase land for the new Pilot Mountain State Park. Using grants from the North Carolina Land and Water Conservation Fund and private money, Pilot Mountain became a state park in 1968. The admission charge was immediately abolished. Five years later, the park removed the staircase to the top of Big Pinnacle. The Yadkin River section of Pilot Mountain State Park was added in 1970, but that's not on the MST.

You'll cross Pinnacle Hotel Road, which separates the Corridor Trail from the mountain section of Pilot Mountain State Park. It climbs the Mountain Trail in the woods to Ledge Spring Trail. Mountain laurel and Catawba rhododendrons bloom together. Huge clumps of Robin's plantain border the trail, but most hikers keep looking up at the huge stone spires. On a dry and warm weekend, climbers hang around the base, waiting for their turn to scale the rocky peaks.

From a distance, Big Pinnacle looks like a wedding cake, with bare rock walls and a rounded top covered by vegetation. Jomeokee Trail encircles Big Pinnacle in less than a mile. The trail is technically not part of the MST, but it's the most popular trail in the park. How could anyone skip it? The rocks towering above hikers are truly awesome. If you look carefully just off the trail toward the Big Pinnacle side, you'll see how people used to climb to the top of Big Pinnacle. The MST reaches the upper parking lot, where tourists wander from viewpoint to viewpoint.

The MST goes down Grindstone Trail, a wide old road where climbers have set up ropes for their colleagues below on Ledge Spring Trail. Then after squeezing between two campsites, the trail continues past the park office. The MST uses Grassy Ridge Trail to leave the park and start on the Sauratown Trail.

# SAURATOWN TRAIL:
## USING PRIVATE LANDS FOR PUBLIC GOOD

The MST goes through the Sauratown Mountains, an isolated mountain range. Sometimes these rocky humps are called the "mountains away from the mountains" because they aren't connected to the Blue Ridge. The Sauratowns look almost like Ayers Rock as they rise up from the surrounding countryside.

The 21.7-mile Sauratown Trail connecting Pilot Mountain State Park to Hanging Rock State Park dates back to 1979. An informal history explains that this trail is the first public hiking and horse trail in North Carolina created on private land.

R.M. Collins, an assistant principal at a local elementary school, and Emily Grogan, a teacher at the same school, both owned horses. "Hikers always wanted to connect the two Sauratown parks," Grogan recalls. With help from other volunteers in the area, they knocked on doors of over thirty-five landowners. They explained their dream of a horse trail and secured a handshake agreement. And it worked. After the trail opened to the public, it was used by hundreds of equestrians and hikers. Nevertheless, erosion and a few careless users concerned the volunteers and landowners. According to Emily, "There wasn't enough protection for the landowners. The liability laws in North Carolina at the time didn't shield landowners from potential problems." The group took down the markers and closed the trail in 1985.

Three years later, the liability laws changed and volunteers organized to start all over again. The horse riders reconnected with all those landowners. They formed the Sauratown Trails Association (STA) and met around kitchen tables, getting reacquainted and, in many cases, meeting for the first time since some of the land had changed hands. This time the landowners signed a ten-year lease agreement.

Emily explains that people who live in the area are the ones who need to approach landowners. "If you're not one of us, if you're not from around here, you don't stand a chance with landowners. They'll think that you're trying to take away their land." STA visited some landowners over five times before they signed on to let the trail go through their private property. But the STA was successful, and in 2002, the Sauratown Trail became part of the MST. Could using private land be a model for other parts of the MST that are now on the road?

Maintaining the Sauratown Trail isn't easy. Like any trail, you need to remove encroaching weeds and trees obstructing the path and put up signs. But a horse trail erodes faster than a hiker-only trail. In some places, people dump garbage—couches, metal appliances and beds—that is almost impossible for volunteers to remove.

Grogan emphasizes that their relationship with landowners is ongoing. The STA has an annual landowner appreciation day. "I check on my landowners. If an elderly owner needs a tree cut down, we do it. It never hurts to be neighborly." Younger people may not be as quick to share their land with the trail. Yet some new owners bought their property just to be close to the trail and will allow the trail to go through their land.

The Sauratown Trail is subdivided into sixteen sections for safety reasons. All but one section is accessible from a road, enabling casual hikers to walk just a small piece and then walk back. Posts have been placed at each section line, with the section number and mileage on each. At first glance, the Sauratown Trail may look like nondescript scrub, but a little further looking reveals a great deal of wildness. Pines, rhododendrons and mountain laurel dominate the landscape. In early March, trout lilies and bluets take advantage of the moisture around creeks. Club moss and American holly keep the trail green year-round.

## The Rock House, a Revolutionary War Fort

The Sauratown Trail crosses small rural roads, passing ponies, old tobacco barns and a large deer stand. The MST always seems to reveal historical gems. Finding the Rock House just off the trail is an exciting surprise. John Martin, a young man originally from Virginia, started building a house from quartzite rock, off what is now Rock House Road. He began the house in 1770, when he was only fourteen years old, just as the rebellion against the British Crown was brewing. Colonists pushed for independence, yet plenty of residents were still loyal to King George III.

The Patriots recognized Martin as a leader. As a soldier, he got around. First, he was part of Rutherford's Expedition to exterminate the Cherokee Indians in 1776. He fought against the Tories when they hid in what is now Tories Den at Hanging Rock State Park. Finally, he was one of the Overmountain Men at the Battle of Kings Mountain, south of Charlotte.

When finished in 1785, the house was an enormous three-story structure with a full basement. It served as a home for his wife and ten children and doubled as a local fort. The walls are three feet thick, and when the roof was on, the house must have been over thirty feet high. Now some walls are missing, and several archways are visible from outside the fence. What's left of the structure is falling apart, making it look like a forgotten British abbey after the Protestant Reformation. Stokes County Historical Society owns the property. A high metal fence surrounds the house to protect it from further damage. The building is not stable, so "Watch out for falling rock" signs are posted all over the ruins.

The Rock House dates back to before the Revolutionary War.

Martin and his wife, Nancy Shipp, are buried on Rock House Road in a small roadside cemetery, close to their house. Nancy's gravestone identifies her first as sister of Thomas Shipp and second as wife of John. This order of the relationship—sister, then wife—is odd. Now there's a mystery.

## HANGING ROCK STATE PARK AND THE LAST WATERFALL ON THE MST

The trail enters Hanging Rock State Park, one of the highlights of the MST. A side trail to Tory's Den leads to a cave and waterfall. During the 1770s, many altercations occurred between Tories, British sympathizers, and Whigs, American Patriots who wanted independence from the Crown. Stokes County was the western edge of the thirteen colonies where Whigs outnumbered Tories. Colonel John Martin became a young leader of the Patriots.

A cave dubbed Tory's Den was home to about one hundred British sympathizers who lost their property to the Whigs. As the story goes, the skirmish occurred one night in 1778 when Tories raided Martin's Rock House and stole supplies. There's a myth that they kidnapped Martin's daughter, but that can't be true since Martin didn't marry and start having children until after the Revolutionary War. The next morning, Martin divided his men into three companies and placed them in different spots

Tories Den in Hanging Rock State Park. How could all those men fit in the cave?

around Tory's Den. The three groups attacked the cave simultaneously and imprisoned most of the residents. The Patriots didn't lose a single man. The trail leads down on elaborate steps to a split between a waterfall and the cave. Tory's Falls has a drop of about fifty feet with a series of cascades below. The cave isn't deep, and you can't go very far without crawling in. The cave was probably used as their headquarters and storage area while the men took shelter around the area.

Back on the MST, the white circles follow Moore's Wall Loop Trail. The trail climbs steadily first through the forest and then turns rocky. Boulders and rock walls make this a captivating section. An outcropping looks like a tower or a finger in space. The view is phenomenal from every overlook.

Moore's Knob at 2,600 feet above sea level is the highest point in Hanging Rock State Park. An observation deck allows for a 360-degree view. It's possible to see the skyline of Winston-Salem below and Big Pinnacle in Pilot Mountain looking northwest. From the top, you can see the Blue Ridge Mountains. When MST hikers reach Moore's Knob, they realize, again, that the trail will only go down from here. This is the last spot that you can call a mountain.

The trail comes down on beautifully crafted stone steps and skirts the lake to the visitor center parking lot. At the visitor center, pictures show the Civilian Conservation Corps boys of Camp #3422 building the mile-long road into the park. Cascade Creek was dammed to create a swimming lake.

From the parking lot, the trail leads down to a waterfall. But before you get to enjoy the waterfall, you have to read the standard state park warning sign: "Warning. This area contains hazards associated with water, rocks and cliff faces. Serious injury or death possible."

What if they said, "Welcome to your state park. Don't climb up the waterfalls because you'll get hurt." The park system scares visitors about all the terrible things that can happen in the woods. No wonder parents want to keep their children inside.

Window Falls is the last true waterfall on the MST. East of here, the land is just too flat. The window is a small hole through a rock, created by water freezing and thawing. Less than two miles from the visitor center, the MST is out of the park and on Hanging Rock Road.

## Musings on Private Land

The Piedmont, in French, means "foothills," not "flat." Hanging Rock Road has steep ups and down. You're forced onto a narrow strip of grass between the road and a ditch. The safest thing might be to cross and recross the road depending on which side has more room to walk on.

The road enters Danbury, an attractive, one-main-street town. The welcome sign proclaims that it's a National Historic District, but its churches are small boxes without steeples, unlike the elaborate Catholic or Episcopalian churches that *look* historic. Whippoorwill Inn, just off the main street, is a good place to stay. The inn consists of two private houses, each with kitchens, cable TV and all the comforts of home. Located on a small back street, it faces an abandoned jail, a fire station and a "pretrial release and district resource center"—i.e., a detention center for wayward boys.

Past the town limit sign, the Danbury Grill with a couple gas pumps is a welcome respite. This MST section goes from gas station to gas station. Gas stations are useful on the road because they offer a place for snacks, garbage cans and comfort stops. It's not as convenient to pop behind a tree while walking the road as it is in the woods.

NC 89 is a mecca for motorcycles: two wheelers, three wheelers, riders alone and riders in packs. They pour out of side roads like creeks flowing into a river. A couple on a Harley honk at hikers in solidarity. You'll walk past broken-down wooden shacks and trailers, substantial manufactured homes and a few brick houses. Weeds cover up abandoned stores. In his guidebook, Scot Ward calls Whickers Grocery a "must stop with very cool people." The store has a Facebook page, so that's cool. Or maybe it's because of the two good-looking young women who staff the store.

Walnut Cove on NC 89 is a sad-looking town with many old, poorly maintained and empty buildings. Fowler Park in front of the library is the only bright spot, even with a state liquor store next door. This section may not be an outstanding part of the MST, but it's the trail, so there's no decision about walking it. Walking is the right pace to see North Carolina and appreciate what's on the road. The trail continues through town and turns on NC 65 toward Stokesdale.

After leaving Walnut Cove, you pass undeveloped land, punctuated by a few single-family homes. Why is the MST on the road? What are people doing with their property? Why doesn't the MST go through this land? The simple answer is that the parcels are privately owned. But these owners aren't doing anything with their land. The first section has been clear cut.

It's a flat mess of stumps and downed saplings, which looks terrible. Maybe the owners hoped to build houses. The parcel is for sale, but if no one wants to buy the land, it's priceless or perhaps just worthless. Other sections are tired, rough woods, with small skinny trees. The land was logged in the past, but nothing has been replanted. A collection of old farm equipment takes up an empty lot. In between, there are a few neat houses with large lawns.

Most of this land isn't used for farming, grazing, playing or living. What if the landowners gave a right of way to the MST? The owners could create a conservation easement or, even better, just donate the land to the state. Much of this land is full of garbage and old abandoned barns about to fall down. Numerous posted and private signs have been nailed to trees. No one is rushing to buy this acreage and build a house on it.

It's easy to blame the poor economy, but this looks like a long-standing problem. The area doesn't attract vacationers or second-home owners because it's not in the mountains and too far from Greensboro. Subdivisions have large cleared swatches of flat land, waiting for houses. An "Under Contract" sign lies on the ground, maybe after the land deal fell apart.

The older generation has lived off this land, and now they want to pass it on. They'll need to divide it among their children, making it even less attractive to potential buyers. Some people have tied up their land in so many legal knots that a real estate lawyer could become cross-eyed. Their children have probably moved away from the region and don't want the hassle of ownership. What would they do with the land?

Even if landowners don't want to let go of their properties, they could get together and allow the MST to come through in an arrangement similar to the Sauratown Trail. However, donating land is not that simple. Some children may want to sell it, others to hold on to it and maybe others would consider giving it away. Why not contact Conservation Trust for North Carolina and let them figure it out? Maybe it's time to reread *A Thousand Acres*.

## THE REVOLUTIONARY WAR IN THE PIEDMONT

Oak Ridge Road heads into Summerfield, a genuine historic town. It passes a memorial to "Bugler Boy" Gillies, who died on this spot at the hands of the British during the Revolutionary War. The small memorial is almost hidden by bushes in front of a power plant. Only a walker can see this plaque, while drivers and cyclists would whizz by without knowing what they missed.

All tales about children killed in war tug at heartstrings, and this one is no exception. Fourteen-year-old James Gillies was the bugler for Lighthorse Harry Lee when he was killed on February 12, 1781, in a skirmish with Tarleton's Dragoons. Even the word "dragoon" conjures up a large and evil man. Dragoons were soldiers who rode horses instead of marching into battle but still fought on the ground.

Closer to the center of Summerfield, a large plaque commemorates Charles Bruce (1733–1832), a Revolutionary War leader and founder of Bruce's Crossroads, now Summerfield. Bruce is buried in a private cemetery under huge trees, along with James Gillies. On the other side of the road, a memorial sits in front of the elementary school. Gillies is also remembered at Guilford Courthouse National Military Park in Greensboro.

A charming historic town like Summerfield should have a café that offers well-made cappuccinos. This café might also let hikers eat their lunch discreetly, but there's nothing on this route. The town hall sits on the corner and welcomes visitors who want to learn more about Bruce and Gillies. Turning the corner, a massive stone house looks like it may have been a small church. Later the MST passes a forlorn shopping center with a large chain drugstore. An antique furniture mall sells couches and easy chairs. It's tempting to sit down and pull out your sandwich, but then you'd really look homeless.

The edges of Summerfield have turned poor and down at the heels. At the Circle M Mobile Trailer Park, the trailers are in bad need of repairs and a good coat of paint. The trailer park has all the classic characteristics of a rural slum. It's on the outskirts of town, out of sight, without any stores close by other than one shopping center that doesn't seem to have a supermarket. A resident shuffles to his trailer. His dog is barking wildly and going nuts, but at least it's on a leash—thank you, sir! Trailers go on forever until U.S. 220, the road that heads into Greensboro. The MST turns into Strawberry Road on the outskirts of the city where the Greensboro Greenway starts.

The Greensboro Greenway rings around several artificial lakes. Lake Brandt is an 816-acre municipal reservoir, built in 1925. You can fish, kayak and canoe on the lake. The network of trails is just north of Guilford Courthouse National Military Park. After skirting the lake for a few miles, the trail moves to a paved railroad-grade trail on the old Atlantic and Yadkin Railway. This line, completed in 1887, went through Greensboro from Wilmington on the coast to Mount Airy and was active until 1974. Dasani, the bottled water company owned by Coke, put up a bright blue metal picnic table protected by a roofed structure open on the sides. The color is jarring in the woods, but this isn't the wilderness. Walkers and runners use this section of trail.

The trail turns left on Nathanael Greene Trail, named for the general who commanded the Continental army's Southern Department and fought against Lord Cornwallis at Guilford Courthouse. The trail sign misspelled Greene's first name, with an *i* instead of that third *a*. Those putting up the signs could have looked it up or checked with the military park.

On a Saturday, people walk their dogs, or their dogs walk them. Most dogs are not on a leash. At each trailhead, the leash laws are clear, but many owners ignore them. The route takes you out of the watershed and through new housing developments. A billboard shows a young African American couple painting a wall that says, "No Down Payment, No Problem." This subdivision is adding to the housing crisis by encouraging people to buy starter houses without a down payment.

## Sharon McCarthy: Biking the MST Roads

Some MST completers choose to bike the road portion of the trail. Sharon started on her bike after leaving Hanging Rock State Park. The first thing you notice about Sharon is how fair she is, fair as in good-looking and fair as in light, like Nicole Kidman. She has blue eyes, pink skin that freckles easily and shoulder-length blond hair. By adulthood, most people's hair has darkened even if they were blond as children, but Sharon's is slowly moving from blond to white.

Born in Lawrenceville in the Virginia Piedmont, Sharon had a rural childhood. Contrary to popular myths, growing up in the country doesn't mean that you hiked and camped as a kid. "My parents never hiked or camped," Sharon said. "Rural children play outside in an unstructured way."

She went to Virginia Tech, where she met her husband, Jim. Work brought them to Charlotte, where they raised three children. Like a good mom, she enrolled her first daughter in the Girl Scouts.

"My older daughter started scouting in second grade. We did lots of arts and crafts, but I got the girls outside and camping. First, we stayed in cabins at our resident camp. By the next year, we camped in tents." After three years, Sharon became a scout leader. "Then my second daughter came up the ranks, so I was a leader in two troops for a total of fifteen years." Unlike most moms, when her girls graduated out of the Girl Scouts, Sharon stayed to rise in leadership roles.

But her scouting work wasn't enough. "When I turned fifty, there were some big changes in my life. My mom died, and my youngest child was leaving for college," Sharon explains. "I looked into hiking all the trails in the Smokies between my fiftieth and fifty-first birthdays." When she started this hiking project, she got her trail name—"Smoky Scout."

On her fiftieth birthday, she went on a weekend backpacking trip to take in several remote trails in the Smokies north of Hazel Creek, including Cold Spring and Welch Ridge trails. These are not easy trails; her project started with a bang. For a while, Sharon didn't feel comfortable hiking alone, as she imagined bears around every bend. Since she's an organizer and a networker, she went out with Girl Scout leaders, hiking clubs and friends. She finally got the knack of hiking by herself. Because the Smokies contain a network of trails, this project requires a lot of planning to minimize repeating trails. On her fifty-first birthday, she finished her project on Old Sugarlands Trail, an easy trail, with her husband, children and many friends.

Sharon then took on the MST but decided to bike the road sections on the trail. It was going to be faster than walking, and that was important to her. She doesn't think of herself as an expert cyclist. "I was concerned about how well I was geared up for this new adventure," she recalls.

Sharon has a hybrid Fuji Crosstown that she rides on rails-to-trails in her Charlotte neighborhood. Her hybrid would keep her versatile and ease her into road biking.

"Who knows? Maybe the MST may be all I ever do on pavement. Cars make me very nervous."

For this new adventure, she didn't buy special bike shoes and just wore sneakers. Padded black Spandex bike shorts were a necessity, along with a snazzy jersey with pockets across the back to hold all her stuff. A helmet, of course, a rain jacket and fingerless gloves to keep her hands from getting scraped if she fell, and she was ready to go.

Her first bike trip on the MST was from Hanging Rock State Park to the Lake Brandt Greenway, a little over thirty-six miles. How hard can that be? she thought. She did a few training rides with Jim, an expert cyclist. "I know my legs are good for hiking, but does that translate to biking? It sure will be nice to cover three times the distance in one day."

The first Saturday morning, she and Jim headed out in two cars; shuttling is still part of the MST routine. Setting up a bike shuttle takes a lot longer because the end points are three times farther apart. They drove to Greensboro, where they dropped off one car and followed the route backward, making and correcting a few wrong turns. As they approached Hanging Rock State Park, the hills grew taller in Sharon's mind and in reality. She wondered about her ability to do the climbs. But she did fine, though it didn't feel that way while she was pedaling and panting on Hanging Rock Road.

"There were plenty of rolling hills, but I took the climbs slowly in first gear on my hybrid and actually enjoyed myself. The downhills were exhilarating." She encountered more traffic than she had experienced before, but she got used to it. Sharon writes on her blog, "Jim and I worked to stay together so that cars could pass us easily at once rather than passing me and then catching up to and passing Jim. I pulled over once because a car was afraid to pass and there was a line building up behind me. I'm glad I have a rearview mirror on my left handlebar. It gives me a sense of security to see what's coming up behind me. I retained my habit of waving to cars, though not quite as cool as the one-finger-salute that cyclists give to each other."

Then there were dogs. "Dogs could speed me up very quickly. A huge dog, sensing that I was the weakest antelope in the herd, came out of nowhere to chase me. I stood up on the bike and pumped furiously, calling for Jim who circled back to put himself between the beast and me. In less than half a minute it was all over, but it left me rattled."

She recalled another tense encounter that took a lot longer "When Jim was out of sight, a large dirty white mongrel from hell with black gums, pink tongue, yellow teeth and bloodshot eyes blasted from the left side of the road and began the chase. He was very persistent, and there was no way I could outrun him. He sprinted alongside me on his side of the road, yelping and foaming, and whenever he began to cross over in front of my bike, I would yell. He'd go back to his side but continue at my pace, which by this time was lightning speed. It's amazing what adrenaline will do. Cerberus chased me well beyond his property lines, and I'm not sure what made him give up, but I lost a couple of years off my life from the encounter."

Hikers carry snacks and lunch and sit on a log or the ground to eat, but cyclists know to check out and rate roadside cafés. Sharon and Jim ate lunch at BJ's Grill, a southern diner next to the Stokesdale post office.

Her last mile in this section was on Highway 220, a major route into Greensboro, which in hindsight they should have walked. A screaming eighteen-wheeler passed them with inches to spare. "But I learned the lesson of staying steady upright while praying hard."

"I've really enjoyed biking through the small towns in the Piedmont," Sharon reflected. "They have a bit of the Mayberry feeling. Some have lots of empty storefronts like my hometown in Virginia, and I wonder how they make it. I wish we had time for more photos, one of the few drawbacks of biking instead of walking. It feels so good pedaling that you don't want to stop."

Sharon continues to hike. She writes, "The walk in the woods on the MST was wonderful, reminding me that this is truly what I love. Road walking is better than sitting on the couch, road biking is tough and exhilarating, but hiking on a trail is just this side of heaven."

## GLENCOE MILL:
## "I OWE MY SOUL TO THE COMPANY STORE"

Glencoe Village, a resurrected historic village located north of Burlington on NC 62, may be the highlight of the Piedmont section of the MST. In 1880, a mill and surrounding village was built on the east bank of the Haw River, one of the last water-powered mills in the area. Since the water available from the Haw River couldn't support a number of mills in one location, each owner built mills on isolated sites. Entire villages were erected to attract, house and support millworkers and their families.

The myth that all textile mills moved to the South from the Northeast persists, but Glencoe Mill was started by James and William Holt, sons of the southern textile pioneer E.M. Holt. A grand Victorian house belonging to one of the owners still stands facing NC 62 before you turn into the village. The success of the Holt fortune can be traced back to 1853, when a French dyer showed one of the Holt sons the fundamentals of mixing dyes. The Holts and Glencoe became famous for their cloth woven with colored stripes, known as Glencoe or Alamance Plaid.

For many workers and their families, Glencoe Village was a transition from farm work to factory with regular hours and regular wages. Single women and widows needing to provide for themselves and their families first migrated to the mills. In *Like a Family: The Making of a Southern Cotton Mill World*, Hall and her colleagues explain that the first generation of men to come off the land in the 1880s found it particularly difficult to adapt to the regimen of factory labor. On the farm, they had exercised authority over their families. They were the ones responsible for the success of the crops. When these men became mill hands, they lost much of that freedom and became subordinate to supervisors and owners. Families held on to some of their rural ways by tending vegetable gardens and keeping chickens and livestock behind their houses. Mill villages were located in rural areas to avoid city taxes and laws. Glencoe Village is still outside the Burlington city limits.

# Walking a Thousand Miles through Wilderness, Culture and History

In *Growing Up in Glencoe,* Billie W. Phillips explains that employees worked eleven hours a day, six days a week. In the 1890s, men doing skilled work were paid two dollars a day while women received one dollar a day. Houses were rented by the room and went for twenty-five to fifty cents per room per month. It's hard to believe now, but millworkers hired black servants. African American women took care of the homes and children of white workers. The mill employed white workers for all but the most menial jobs.

The mill village was run on a classic paternalistic system, and the Baptist owners felt responsible for their workers' behavior. Since millworkers didn't have their own transportation, the owner provided a church, Union Chapel, meant for all denominations. The village was split between Baptists and Methodists. Later, a Baptist church was built, which still stands. The supervisor had police powers. His house was located at the entrance to the village so he could see what was going on. Workers who misbehaved could be evicted. And then where would they go, and how would they get there?

By the 1900s, textile mills started relocating from the Northeast to the South, where the workforce was cheaper and non-unionized. Massachusetts passed a forty-hour workweek law in 1919, which spurred mills to move south. The peak year was in 1935, when the companies left ghost towns in the Northeast where mills had previously thrived.

Glencoe Mill operated continuously until 1954. Once the mill closed, the village was abandoned and the houses deteriorated. Even after the site was added to the National Register of Historic Places, the area was used as a dumping ground. In 1997, Preservation North Carolina bought some of the property from the heirs of the mill owners. Sarah Rhyne, the other part owner, understood the historic significance of the site and donated her share. At the time, thirty-five houses were still standing. Unlike most mill villages, Glencoe was never subdivided.

Slowly, people bought into Glencoe Village, restored their homes and moved in, but no one can mistake the two streets for a typical suburb. In 1998, Hank and Lynn Pownell purchased the first house. Like most houses in the development, theirs had no electricity, plumbing or central heating. The Pownells are originally from Minneapolis but visited North Carolina many times. One day, Lynn saw a tiny article about the restoration at Glencoe Village.

"We drove here from the Triangle, and I fell in love with the houses. We wanted a two-story house with a south-facing porch. At the time, twenty houses on Glencoe Street were for sale. The restoration took a lot longer than Preservation North Carolina anticipated...I think this is the best house on the street, but everyone thinks that their house is the best."

Lynn and Hank bought a four-room dwelling and started major renovations. "It's a good place to live. I'm a weaver," Lynn said. "The whole idea of using the detached kitchen as a studio was important. I find the history of textile really exciting."

After Lynn and Hank moved in, it took a period of adjustment—"Honey, what do we talk about now?"—but Lynn and Hank both agree that their house will never be finished. Lynn loves the quiet of the area but admits that she misses the excitement of the city. "If I could have a getaway place, it would be a condo in a city where I could walk to a coffee shop."

"People had trashed the area," Hank explained. "Our house was last occupied in the 1940s." While Lynn still had several years before retirement, Hank managed the renovations. He lived in the old barbershop during his stint as his own general contractor. Now the Pownells rent out the barbershop. The tiny structure has a double bed, kitchen and bathroom. Though it's a small place for two guests, the owners have managed to make it comfortable. Billie Phillips also remembers the barbershop, with two chairs for waiting customers but no running water. The barber lived where he worked. A bed had been shoved in a corner, with an oil stove and lamp.

Glencoe Mills obtained cotton from eastern North Carolina in five-hundred-pound bales. The cotton was already ginned—that is, cleaned of seeds and other debris. The former company office and store is now a Textile Heritage Museum, open only Saturdays and Sundays for a few hours. The museum is filled with pictures, mill equipment and paraphernalia. A loom, knitting machine and circular knitting machine are squeezed in the small room.

Jerrie Nall, the museum director, interprets the exhibits. "When you ask someone how they're doing, they might say 'Fair to middling,'" Jerrie says. "Well, that's a textile grading expression." She points to a tall vertical cabinet with many drawers, each labeled with the quality of the cloth inside. The next room displays products from contemporary American mills. Dye Lock makes fabric sheets, which you throw in a washing machine to prevent a garment from bleeding its color on other pieces. Wright socks prevent blisters, and Glen Raven makes specialty fabrics, including parachutes and astronaut suits.

Lynn has leased the old Glencoe Mill machine shop opposite the museum and is repurposing the building as an artist's studio. She'll move her weaving studio from her house to Glencoe Studios, where she'll have more room. Several other artists have committed to work here as well. They plan to give classes on their particular craft, such as weaving, painting and sculpting. But to attract artists and art lovers, you need to provide them with food and good coffee. Lynn dreams of a restaurant by the Haw River, as well as a café. In a few years, Glencoe Village will be a destination for art lovers and gourmet eaters.

The mill itself has yet to be renovated. It would make a great umbrella for shops, offices and restaurants, but the huge brick building is deteriorating. With a few stores and meeting space, Glencoe Village might be a walkable town, but for now, residents have to get into their cars to find a coffee shop or a container of milk.

Textile mills have not completely disappeared in North Carolina. The 1979 movie *Norma Rae* tells a modern story of a textile mill in the eastern part of the state. Sally Fields plays the title role of a millworker who's encouraged to become a union leader. It's a very stereotypical story. A Jewish union worker comes down from Brooklyn to a small southern town to unionize the mill. The bosses have to put up with him, but they don't have to cooperate.

The mill is deafeningly loud, even when the workers take their breaks. Since everyone must wear earplugs, the employees can't talk to one another while they work. Cotton flies around and lands everywhere. It's taken a toll on the employees' lungs. Unlike Glencoe Mill of the past, this mill is fully integrated. While the bosses try to create some division between African American and white workers, they're not successful; millworkers are connected by their misery in the plant. To break the threat of unions, Norma Rae is promoted to spot checker, but it doesn't last long.

"They're watching me. They're watching you," Norma Rae tells the co-worker whose work she's now checking. The story occurred in 1973 to Crystal Lee Sutton, the real Norma Rae, in Roanoke Rapids, North Carolina. She didn't "live happily ever after" when the union came to the J.P. Stevens mills. She was fired from the mill and took on a series of jobs worse than her millwork until she became a union spokesperson and later a nursing assistant. She died of brain cancer at age sixty-eight.

## Emily's Cookies, a Welcome Stop

Hikers usually want to stop at the top of a long uphill for a breather, but if the trail is gentle, there are no external clues to take a break. On the road, it's tempting to just walk and walk without a rest. The trail passes Reedy Fork Organic Farm, which produces milk for Organic Valley Milk. In Ossipee, the Old Ski Lodge has never seen a skier; it's a bar. Hikers can sit on a bench in front to eat and read all the warning signs they've put up:

*No club colors on premises*
*No ID, no beer*
*All beer bought to go must leave premises*
*No smoking inside as of 01-02-2010*
*No firearms allowed on premises*

On Sundays, guys sit in their cars or on motorcycles waiting for the noon hour, when the bar can open. If you're looking for a restroom on the side of the building, keep reading the signs: "Door is bolted" and "Please use restrooms inside." So go inside, and you'll find a friendly bartender who'll point you to the right place.

Emily's Cookies, a plain boxy building, sits on a corner of Jeffries Cross Road. It offers a couple of outdoor tables to enjoy a snack. Debra Malchow owns Emily's Cookie Mix Shoppe with her husband, Craig, in the proverbial "middle of nowhere" north of Glencoe Village. Without any other businesses around, it's a welcome stop for MST hikers. The display case offers cookies, fruit bars and pastries that she bakes in the back of the store. She sells ice cream and coffee and carries a few gift items around the corner. There's just enough room for five tables on the side of the shop. Debra, wearing a long red apron, has such an infectious warm personality that she'd be a success no matter what she did or where she did it.

So if the owner is not Emily, who is? Debra points to a small picture of a little toddler on the counter. Though it's only a headshot, you can see that Emily's head is bigger than her body and her ears stick out. The little girl looks dazed.

"This is my daughter Emily," Debra says. "She was born with a genetic disorder called Trisomy-18. It means that there's extra material from chromosome 18." Debra and Craig are former Wisconsinites and have the broad nasal accents to prove it. They moved from Hudson on the St. Croix River when Craig took a position at Procter & Gamble in Greensboro. Debra was a typical mom with two boys.

When Emily was born, the doctors gave her five days to live. She had open-heart surgery when she was four days old and had a shunt put in. This gave her a chance to live a little longer and to make her life a bit easier. She would be a teenager now.

"We were determined to bring her home and care for her. We were told that we wouldn't be able to do it, that she belonged in a hospital. But we found Kids Path, a hospice for children, and we got a lot of help. Emily survived until she was two." Debra tears up when she explains that Emily needed an oxygen tube twenty-four hours a day, seven days a week.

"Her oxygen tubes had to be changed and cleaned. She needed eight medications a day. Her lungs had to be cleared out. We did chest exercises. When I first brought her home, she took in a drop of milk at a time. Nurses from the university trained me. After that, we just gave her love."

It must be so discouraging to care for a child, knowing that she's going to die. Debra seems in such good spirits. "I started Emily's Cookies to honor my miracle daughter."

Debra made cookies while she was home caring for Emily. The women who helped her would rave about her baking. After Emily died, she and Craig started with a chocolate chip cookie mix, which they offered on the web. Instead of putting all the ingredients in one bag, her mix comes in three separate bags. Debra tests out her many mixes in the back room. Some people said, "But we don't bake," so she started baking cookies as well.

They opened a shop in a strip mall in downtown Burlington. "When we needed to move, this property became available. We wanted to be practical. We live a mile away," Debra recalls. The building was a house, which they remodeled into a bakery and coffee shop. There's nothing out here other than gas stations. Debra holds cookie-decorating classes and bakes wedding cakes. "It took a while, but people now know us."

Craig works for Debra. "I have two part-time employees, so I could use Craig in the business. Everything happens for a reason," Debra says. She wants to continue talking about Emily.

"Kids Path in Alamance County was started in early 2000. They help families who want to keep their child at home. It also helps with the grieving process." But how did this affect their other children? "Brandon was only in the first grade," Debra says. "He never said a bad word about Emily, and he doesn't want anyone to forget her. Our older one was more reserved. We were all together and focused on what was important. When Chloe was born, she blended in with the rest of the family. It was no big deal." Chloe, now thirteen, was born while Emily was still alive. "Emily must have said, 'You have Chloe now. I can go back to the Lord.'" Religion sustains Debra and Craig.

The dogs are the one drawback to this great trail stop. A mean-looking dog wanders the area to invade the private space of Emily's Cookies. The mutt has short, stubby legs and a growling attitude, just the kind of dog that you'd want to abandon. On the road, a can of pepper spray in your hand or pocket, not stashed in your pack, is a good idea, just in case.

On the hill diagonally opposite Emily's Cookies, a pack of aggressive dogs waits for walkers and cyclists. The dogs bark and excite one another. More dogs charge down the embankment. Several more dogs pace back and forth, trying to decide if they want to come down and add to the chaos. What's the matter with these owners?

"The neighbors used to be friendly, but their house was broken into and they got dogs," Debra shakes her head. "When I tried to talk to them, they said that I was causing problems, so they won't talk to us now. There is a leash law in Alamance County, but the attitude is 'You're not in the city. Deal with it.' I won't call animal control because I don't blame the dogs. As a business, you don't want conflict with your neighbors."

The ice cream isn't rich, and the coffee might not be as strong as at Starbucks, but it's not about the food at Emily's Cookies. It's about Debra, Craig and Emily's memory. If you pass by when the store is open, stop in to say hello and put a couple dollars in the Kids Path collection jar.

## REACHING THE ENO RIVER

The road walk takes the MST hiker from farm to farm. On Schley Road, the horsy set owns large tracts of land. A few pampered horses stick their heads out of the fence, looking for handouts. Many barns, some with three stories, appear larger than most town houses. One horse with a black forehead and ears looks like it's wearing earmuffs. The houses are large and set back, but there are no menacing dogs or "Private Property—Keep Out" signs. The richer the area, the fewer warning signs you'll see.

After St. Mary Road, the road changes character again. Horses have disappeared, the lots are heavily wooded and the houses are smaller. In front of a corner house, a mannequin sits wearing noise-canceling earphones. Another spot has several wreaths made up of plastic flowers, with ten memorials on the side of the road. A van full of people may have swerved around the curve and hit a tree, killing everyone inside.

Pleasant Green Road bisects Eno River State Park, and the MST in the park is in the eastern section. The trail starts flat and in a mile and a half reaches a quarry. In the early 1960s, rocks from this area were used to build I-85, which passes close by. When construction on the interstate ended, the quarry gradually filled with water and a four-acre pond was created. The scene here is idyllic. A few people swim. Others lay around

Starting on Clingmans Dome in Great Smoky Mountains National Park.

In Nantahala National Forest, the trail goes through an open meadow, not typical of the mountains.

Skinny Dip Falls in the Pisgah District, but sorry, everybody has clothes on.

Gray's lilies, a rare flower, endemic to the Southern Appalachians.

Purple-fringed orchids can be
seen at high altitude.

Coming down from Mount
Mitchell, the highest point on the
MST. *Courtesy of Sharon McCarthy.*

*Above*: Crossing the Linville
River. *Courtesy of Sharon
McCarthy.*

*Left*: Walking across a
waterfall is always a
challenge, but that's where
the trail goes.

Hunt Fish Falls in Wilson Creek feels very remote.

From the Tanawha Trail, you can see the iconic Linn Cove Viaduct on the Blue Ridge Parkway.

The Blue Ridge Parkway allows grazing on its land because it was a historic practice.

Flat Top Manor, the summer home of Moses and Bertha Cone, now houses the Parkway Craft Center.

Through the meadows and bluffs of Doughton Park. *Courtesy of Sharon McCarthy.*

Stone Mountain rises seven hundred feet from the valley floor.

The wedding cake formation of Big Pinnacle in Pilot Mountain State Park.

From Moore's Wall in Hanging Rock State Park.

A house in Glencoe Mill Village, as found in 1998. *Courtesy of Lynn Pownell.*

The same house when the new owners moved in several years later.

On the Haw River.

You need to stay visible when you're walking the road.

Many modern artifacts remain in Falls Lake Recreation Area left by those who lived here before the area was flooded.

Falls Lake.

Main Street, Youngsville, in Franklin County. *Courtesy of Kate Dixon.*

Colorful rocking chairs on La Grange's Main Street.

Tryon Palace in New Bern.

The beginning of the Neusiok Trail in Croatan National Forest.

Characteristic swamp on the Neusiok Trail.

Some MST completers decide to ride the road portions of the trail. *Courtesy of Sharon McCarthy.*

*Right*: Kite and owner on
the beach.

*Below*: A painter has settled
on the beach at Pea Island
National Wildlife Refuge,
oblivious to the blazing sun.

On the beach at Cape Hatteras National Seashore.

Sand dunes in Jockey's Ridge State Park.

A pampered horse in Durham still looks for a handout.

the water reading and eating. Even though the banks seem flat, kids find a way to jump in.

Huge obligatory warning signs have been placed on both sides of the approach to the quarry, so visitors can see them, no matter how they get here. You need to be vigilant because you'll hit deep water immediately. Submerged trees and rocks are hidden in the water. Maybe construction equipment lies below as well. The sign says that swimming is not recommended, not that it's forbidden.

Past the quarry, tourists walk toward you, looking like they're heading to the beach. They've started from one of several parking areas closer than the one on Pleasant Green Road. People wear slippers, flip-flops, flimsy sandals or boots without socks. Some are just in their bathing suits, carrying towels, beach toys and bottles of water. Locals walk from their houses.

The trail follows the river and then swerves away up on a high bank, only to come down again—up and down, several times. The Eno River is a slow river full of large rocks and vegetation that sticks out of the water. In some places, you'd expect a crocodile to rear its head. Plenty of mountain laurel borders the trail but no rhododendrons. In mid-summer, larkspur, bowman's root, jewelweed and small coneflowers bloom. In the spring, trillium, wild geraniums and irises grow along the trail. Most flowers are familiar to those who've walked the mountain trails, but then there's the native swamp rose, a tall shrub with pale pink petals. Here, you're almost at sea level.

The Eno River Task Force built this new piece of trail to connect to Pump Station Trail. True to its name, the trail has the remains of a pump station. From 1887 to 1927, the Eno River provided Durham with its water, but it won't again. The city wanted to build a reservoir, but residents organized and led a campaign to preserve the Eno River Valley. Concerned locals like Margaret Nygard created the Eno River Association to protect the river from being dammed up. Freshwater mussels and turtles are found in the water. Shells cover the ground close to the river.

The crumbling walls and remnants of a holding tank for the old water supply clash with trees, ferns and vines. Metal screws and engine parts stick out of the ground. Poison ivy covers the brick structures, and that may be the best protection from vandals. An old well has a tree growing from its center. Dappled light makes for poor photos, and the walls almost blend into the scenery.

Laurel Bluff Trail parallels the river. Many sturdy wooden bridges have been built over dry side streams. The trail has more bridges than necessary, but that's a state park for you. Many access points allow visitors to put their feet in the water. The trail passes the chimney and foundation of an old hunting lodge and the Guess Mill Dam.

Crossing Guess Road is jarring and dangerous. Cars whizz through the four-lane suburban road, not expecting hikers. Across the road, the trail follows a driveway behind a small brick building, which houses the Eno River Association and ends by crossing the Eno River on a huge metal bridge.

Hikers on a schedule may be tempted to just blow past West Point on the Eno, a Durham city park, but the remains of the old West Point community deserve some time and attention. The park, opened in 1976, now has four hundred acres. Though small, it's well loved and managed.

With warm summer weather, the park attracts day camps for inner-city kids—kids in the water, kids on the lawn, kids running around, kids eating a snack before quiet time and going home. The children are not put off by the sign at the entrance of the accessible section of river, which says in large capital letters: "DO NOT DISTURB THE SNAKES." It goes on to explain that there are no venomous snakes in the Eno River.

Over thirty flour, textile and gristmills used the Eno River from the mid-1700s to the early 1900s. A mill was not just a place to grind flour. Locals gathered at the mill to meet, shop and share the latest gossip. The West Point community was the largest and busiest along the river.

Several historical structures are clustered together near the river, including a reconstructed mill. In 1942, a deluge took apart the dam, and the mill building collapsed, probably from old age and neglect. But Eno supporters were determined to rebuild and reopen the mill. And today, the mill is grinding corn and wheat with water power.

The Hugh Mangum Photographic Museum is another success story in the history of preserving community stories. Hugh Mangum (1877–1922) grew up in Durham. The Mangum house on the park property was the family summer home and later their permanent home. Hugh Mangum became an itinerant photographer, wandering the South looking to photograph people.

"He was fascinated by the lyrical, beautiful and extravagant in everyday life," reads a museum sign. And he could afford to be. When he ran out of money, Mangum came back home for a resupply of cash.

He took over the second floor of the Mangum Packhouse, where tobacco was sorted and graded. The building has now been turned into the museum. Since roll film was not yet available, Mangum used dry glass plates. The museum displays several of Mangum's large format cameras, as well as his personal effects, such as a shaving kit and the family Bible, along with a wicker posing chair where he asked his subjects to sit. Mangum recorded his trips with the date and location on his traveling trunk. You'd think that he would have used a notebook, but a notebook would have disappeared. Photographs show Mangum with wire-rim glasses and always wearing a jacket.

Samples of his photographs are hung on the second floor, mostly of people that he encouraged to pose, including a few African Americans. All were very formally dressed. Visitors can peek into the tiny darkroom. Duke University, which holds Mangum's glass plates, is reprinting the photographs. He died of pneumonia in 1922 when he was forty-four. His brother, Leo, lived in the house until 1966, so the property wasn't vacant for long.


## FALLS LAKE STATE RECREATION AREA: SIXTY MILES OF TRAIL IN THE TRIANGLE

A few miles of road walking takes hikers to Penny's Bend Nature Preserve and the start of over sixty miles of trail in Falls Lake Recreation Area. Here, the MST doesn't go through wilderness. What areas east of the Mississippi really are truly wild? The land is restoring itself, and nature is bouncing back.

The Neuse River, formed by the confluence of the Eno River and Flat River in Durham County, stretches 248 miles from the Falls Lake Reservoir Dam to its mouth at Pamlico Sound past New Bern. The Neuse River has several superlatives attached to it. It's the longest river in North Carolina and is contained within the state. At its mouth, it's 6 miles across, the widest river in America. The Neuse is intimately connected with the MST through the Coastal Plains. However, here the trail is all about the lake and the recreation amenities around it. The Army Corp of Engineers dammed up the Neuse River to create Falls Lake.

There's a saying: "Chocolate, chocolate, chocolate—is good vanilla too." The Appalachians were spectacular, but walking Falls Lake offers different scenery with its own charm. This section of trail starts close to Penny's Bend Nature Preserve, worth a detour. The site is only eighty-four acres, but it boasts rare indigenous plants.

From Penny's Bend, the woods are filled with ferns and hardwoods, such as oaks and sweet gum. The trail is so fresh and new that orange flags used to route the trail are still here. Though the trail gets close to water, trees obstruct the fleeting river views. A great blue heron rises out of the water and flies in a high circle, as if to say, "I own this place." The water is still, muddy and full of swamp grass. Islands of stunted trees seem to float in the flood plain.

Several railroads cross the trail. The first set of tracks is abandoned and looks like a nursery log full of plants and trees growing between the rails. Farther on, the Norfolk Southern line spur ends at a finger of the lake. These tracks are clean and probably in working order.

The MST crosses several cleared areas where power lines with double posts stand like guards. The literature explains that "power line easements create an edge effect that attracts animals." Two large osprey nests sit on top of the posts. A stash of moonshine paraphernalia is strewn around at a road crossing. Several large metal barrels and glass mason jars lie helter-skelter close to a dirt road. People may have stayed here overnight because a rusty, open can of beef stew has been left behind. An old metal bed frame lies on its side. But where was the water source? To make moonshine whiskey, you need clear, flowing water. Before the Army Corps of Engineers dammed the Neuse River, small streams may have run a lot more freely.

The Army Corps of Engineers has jurisdiction over all navigable waters. George Washington appointed the first military engineer, and the corps became a permanent part of the army in 1802. But Congress always wanted the corps to work on civilian projects. In modern times, the corps, while responsible for flood control, also provides hydroelectric energy and, not so incidentally, creates opportunities for recreation.

The corps investigated the Neuse River Basin from 1958 to 1964. The study sought solutions to the predictable flooding that ravaged eastern North Carolina, causing millions of dollars in damage. Raleigh was also in dire need of a reliable water source to support the current and future population. The city experienced regular water shortfalls and saw severe droughts in the 1950s. To create the lake, the corps bought close to forty thousand acres from landowners, of which twelve thousand acres are now under water. The dam was completed in 1981.

According to Jeff Brewer, task force leader for Falls Lake of Friends of the MST, the group took seven years to work on a Memorandum of Understanding with the corps and other agency partners and four and a half years to actually build the trail from Penny's Bend Nature Preserve to U.S. 50. From U.S. 50 to the dam, the trail had already been built by the Triangle Greenway Council in the 1980s.

On this stretch of MST, the corps agreed on the general route that the trail should take. Then Jeff and his crew flagged the actual route. Before anyone could start to build the trail, someone from the corps came out to walk the land. The NC Wildlife Commission, the Division of Parks and Recreation and Durham and Wake Counties also had to approve the route details.

At East Geer Street close to tiny Lake Ridge Airport, a flock of meadowlarks flies overhead. On a cold winter day, a finger of Falls Lake has iced over, but that's an unusual event here. Having long left the Appalachian Mountains, the trail is lined by loblolly pines, a southern tree that you don't see in the mountains, and even a couple of small longleaf pines. The terrain is gently undulating but not flat, going up and down about one hundred feet at a time.

Former residents left plenty of artifacts or garbage, depending on how you look at it. Cars, trucks, stoves and even commodes lie forlorn off the trail, probably not worth moving. Washing machines were popular items to ditch. Tobacco barns and old chimneys remain and, at one place, a complete home site with tobacco barn, chicken coops and other outbuildings. Sometimes the route finding is tricky, and MST circles kept disappearing. The lake is not visible all the time, so it's a treat when it appears and a bigger treat with a heron resting on its banks.

The trail goes around fingers of the lake. At Little Lick Creek, Friends of the MST volunteers recently built a beautifully arched bridge. That gets you halfway across the creek onto an island. Floating wooden boardwalks were installed on the other half. But sometimes when there's a lot of rain and the water is two to three feet high, you're wading in the creek. FMST is working out what to do about this and will probably fill in with more boardwalks. Walking around this protrusion of the lake would add five extra miles.

At one point, the trail almost lands in someone's front yard. The homeowners appear to have their own private access to Falls Lake where they've parked a canoe. In reality, the corps has never allowed shoreline permits. With a shoreline permit, a landowner could install floating boat docks, build steps and walkways and remove vegetation along Falls Lake. Though the access to the lake is public, their dogs bark and chase hikers. The dogs don't understand that hikers can walk in front of their master's house.

The trail rolls through loblolly and white pines and tulip trees. Here there's little activity on the lake. Way out in the distance, a boater motors across. The land seemed to be on the way to recovery. With just a cursory look at the scenery, you'd call it scrub. However, within a few miles, if you examine the surroundings a little closer and make a list, you might see a family of deer, toads, butterflies, caterpillars, box turtles, centipedes, grasshoppers, spiders, robins, sparrows, crows, mockingbirds and a lone sandpiper around the bridge. You'll hear a woodpecker and swat at swarming gnats. This is an impressive list, since the land has had a chance to recuperate for only about thirty years.

Bluets are huge, compared to those in the mountains, and blue-eyed grass and blackberry canes are plentiful. A couple of lilies with six white petals and grass-like leaves have popped up in open moist areas. These hardy Zephyr or rain lilies are found along country roads throughout the Coastal Plains of the southeastern United States. The lily was brought to the mountains by the Cherokees, probably for medicinal purposes. It naturalized quite well in the valley wetlands of the Blue Ridge. Because it's now difficult to find in the mountains, Western Carolina University in Cullowhee, close to Sylva, is trying to reestablish the lily on campus and promoting the flower as a Cullowhee lily.

Bluebirds flit about in the scrub and fields, herons sit on the shores of the inlets and gulls fly over the open water. The trail goes past plaques that explain various types of trees, including post oak, Virginia pines and Florida maples. Rolling View Campground, just off the MST, is a luxurious place to camp. Like most campgrounds managed by the NC State Park system, each site has a picnic table, a fire pit with a grill and a tent pad. A bathhouse with hot showers sits in the middle of the campground.

Past Rolling View Marina, the trail enters Wake County through an upscale area and crosses NC 50. No garbage here. The trail goes in and out of the state park and North Carolina Gamelands. There's no concern about getting lost since much of the trail is over ten years old, well marked and patted down by many feet, though some think the signage is excessive. The Friends of the MST trail crew built impressive bridges and staircases. The trail passes several houses, some with mean-sounding dogs. The gunshots you'll hear in the Wildlife Management areas are probably just for target practice, though small game like turkey and grouse can be hunted most of the year. The North Carolina Wildlife Commission keeps the area cut and open to attract deer for hunters and birds for bird enthusiasts. In the mountains, they may not keep up with mowing and tree removal, but here some areas are as smooth as a baby's bottom. There are almost no artifacts on this section, no abandoned houses, cabins or barns, just the Norwood Cemetery, a family plot with three headstones.

Big plans are in store for part of the 586-acre peninsula between Highway 98 and Falls Dam. A master plan for Forest Ridge Park has been on the drawing board for years. Voters approved a 2003 Parks and Recreation Bond Referendum. Later, the Raleigh City Council adopted the master plan, which will include a Welcome Center, an adventure education center, ropes course, lakeside center, multiuse activity areas, an overnight lodge and mountain biking and hiking trails. After an environmental assessment, the corps declared that there were findings of no significant impact, a big step forward, but it will be a while before the public will be able to enjoy all these activities.

You may want to take a short detour to see the Blue Jay Center for Environmental Education, which focuses mostly on school groups. But you're already in the environment. How often can long-distance hikers go off the trail to see something interesting? Obviously they have to pick and choose or else 1,000 miles could end up being 1,200 or more.

The trail goes through coves of holly trees, beech and mountain laurels. In the rain, the rising mist above Falls Lake creates a dreamy picture. The dead end on Bayleaf Church Road is a tourist attraction in itself. The high-end Carlyle housing development has several huge McMansions.

## Falls of the Neuse: Where Are the Falls?

Close to the Falls of the Neuse area, you start to hear traffic. A boardwalk takes you up to a parking area behind the Falls Lake Visitor Assistance Center, run by the Army Corps of Engineers. The building houses a small exhibit that explains the history of Falls Lake. Farther down the trail, a line of longleaf pine trees, the original trees in the area, was planted. Falls of the Neuse has picnic areas, restrooms and parking. The waterfall doesn't really drop like in the Blue Ridge Mountains but creates a tiny riffle by a tailrace out of the lake.

Janet Steddum of Raleigh became fascinated by the Falls community that lived here before the dam was built. She researched the history of the former residents and published *The Battle for Falls Lake*. According to Steddum, the Falls community bore the brunt of the upheaval caused by the construction of the lake. Many locals had heard talk of the possibility of a lake since 1930, but no active organized group focused on saving the area from flooding, as they did at Eno River. Highways, roads, utilities and, of course, cemeteries were relocated to clear the reservoir for flooding. The upper reaches of the Neuse River became Falls Lake. But unlike the people who moved out of Great Smoky Mountains National Park or the Blue Ridge Parkway, this is recent history.

Two hundred families were displaced. Some battled the ridiculously low offers, but there was a rush for land around the proposed lake. Everyone would want to live on the lake. Though most citizens of Raleigh were tired of the predictable droughts and looked forward to a reliable source of water, the Research Triangle Sierra Club opposed the project. Ironically, the extra land around the lake is now protected from future development. The corps did not grant easements here. Old folks couldn't stay in their homes until they died, as they did in Great Smoky Mountains National Park. The corps bought everyone outright, and people had to move.

Some residents welcomed the government buyout. They too were tired of the flooding caused by a heavy rain, which locals called a "frog strangler." Other residents couldn't get enough money from the government to buy an equivalent house and land and settled for a mobile home. Almost no one fought the government.

So where are the falls today? As the Army Corps of Engineer website explains, "The word *falls* refers to the Neuse River's very rocky bottom and the small waterfalls that are in the river below Falls Dam. Unfortunately, the current Falls Dam sits on top of most of those rocks that made up the falls that gives the dam and nearby Falls community their names.

Before the current earth dam, there was a concrete dam and a wooden dam before that. "In fact," Janet explains, "once you put in a dam, any dam, the falls disappear." John Lawson, who wrote *A New Voyage to Carolina*, traveled from the Eno River to the Neuse in 1701. He wrote about the falls, but no one alive today has seen them. The falls are no more.

Steddum explains her fascination with the history of Falls Lake. "I live pretty close to the lake, and I saw things that didn't seem to fit in the forest. There were abandoned cemeteries and remnants of homesteads. People were there and then they weren't. Nature takes over, but if you look closely, you can see human footprints and roads that drop into the lake. People were in the way of progress, but some residents were still alive when I started the project. It was such a thrill for me to interview the locals. I started doing research into the past. I could go back to mid-1600s with written records. The Army Corp of Engineers was instrumental in looking at archaeological sites. I relied on the corps so much."

In 1855, the Falls of the Neuse Manufacturing Company used the powerful falls to produce paper. After changing hands, name and use many times, the Erwin Cotton Mill finally closed in 1959. The buildings were purchased to be used as a cotton warehouse, but the beautiful granite mill deteriorated for decades until it became River Mill Condominiums in 1984 and was placed on the National Register of Historic Properties. Today the three-story stone building with tall vertical windows looks forbidding, like a prison or an old-fashioned cottage hospital. It backs on the Neuse, and residents have put in lounge chairs and a gazebo and built easy access to the river. It must be a good place to live.

Steddum focused on the Falls community because it was the oldest active group before the dam was built. If you want to see a little of what remains of the community, walk past the grocery store on the corner across the street from the Falls parking area and on Fonville Road. The mill supervisors lived on this section of the street, but no workers houses are left, maybe because, unlike Glencoe Village, they just fell apart. The lake devastated the community, and yet it still exists. Many of the original inhabitants didn't move very far. The author keeps in touch with the former residents, but they're dying off. Steddum went to a homecoming to meet some of the people who lived in the Falls community. Old-timers want to speak to her. A woman brought her widowed mother and said, "You wrote the book my father wanted me to write."

# Jeff Brewer, Friends of the MST Activist

Jeff Brewer is probably the person most associated with the MST after Allen de Hart. That's not a coincidence since Allen and Jeff have been working together on the trail for so long. Jeff heads the Friends of the MST task force that built the trail around Falls Lake in Durham and Raleigh.

Jeff Brewer at a Falls Lake workday. *Courtesy of Jeff Brewer.*

"It took four and a half years to build thirty-three miles. We finished in 2010. Sometimes, over 150 people came out on a workday. After one workday was over, it was time to plan for the next time. Now we have five maintenance days a year.

"Our section maintainers on Falls Lake are organized like in Carolina Mountain Club. They keep their piece of trail open and clean. They need to be the eyes and ears of their sections. I walk other people's sections when they can't do it. I keep emphasizing that you need to be walking your section. All together, we maintain over sixty miles of trail, and I organize the workdays."

Jeff was born in Wilmington, on the North Carolina coast, and moved to Durham when he was in eighth grade. "My dad gave me one of Allen's books. He also told me that one day there will be a hiking trail through North Carolina." By then Jeff had done some backpacking on the A.T. with the Boy Scouts.

Jeff's father was a student in Allen's class at Louisburg College. "I went to Louisburg College, where I met Allen de Hart. My father pointed out that I could take backpacking as my physical education requirement in college. And he said, 'By the way, son, the book I gave you on North Carolina trails? That was written by the prof who teaches the backpacking courses.'"

Jeff started Louisburg College in 1996. He worked in Allen's gardens, a small private nature preserve open to the public. He also went on trips to help Allen with his hiking guides.

"One weekend, we drove from Pilot Mountain to Wake Forest to come up with a road route for the MST. I was the scribe in the truck and filled a yellow legal pad of instructions. My hand was stiff after that weekend."

When the MST seemed to be forgotten by the state of North Carolina, Allen discussed his plans to start Friends of the MST, a nonprofit organization to keep the momentum of the MST going. Allen wanted Jeff to help.

"What does it entail?" Jeff wanted to know. "Oh, just a little work," Allen said. "And by the way, I want you to be president of Friends of the MST."

When Jeff started NC State, he found himself running a nonprofit out of his dorm room. "We had an answering machine," Jeff recalls, "but instead of having a message, like 'Hey, let's party on Friday evening,' we kept it very professional—'You've reached the office of Friends of the MST.'

"Allen took Friends of the MST seriously, and so did I. I put in many hours and learned a lot. I was president from 1997 to 2009. When I finally stepped down, my e-mail went down by 75 percent." In 2003, Jeff hiked the MST. "I needed to see the whole trail for myself and took a leave of absence from work."

Jeff explained that there's still one man who's bitter about having to sell some of his land to the Army Corp of Engineers. He didn't think he got paid enough for his land. When people moved out, they left mattresses, stoves and trucks. So when are the objects considered garbage, and when are they considered artifacts?

"When we're cleaning the trail from 9:00 a.m. to 3:00 p.m., the stuff is garbage. After 3:00 p.m., it's an artifact. But sometimes," Jeff explains, "our maintenance crew can't even pull out tires from the lake. Tires are turned in to the North Carolina Wildlife Resources Commission for recycling, and sometimes the commission doesn't have the money to pay recyclers to get rid of the tires."

During the week, Jeff is a partner in a small company that removes asbestos. "We do mostly popcorn ceilings and kitchen floor." His wife, Amy, works at a major software company in the Triangle. "We went to high school together and then reconnected." They have a daughter, Lalen, and a black and white cat called Mister Tuxedo, Tux for short.

Jeff loves the outdoors and has big hiking plans. "Not having showers is the pain you endure to see things," Jeff says. "I want to finish the A.T. from Harpers Ferry to Georgia in sections. Then when I retire, I'll go from Harpers Ferry north to Maine. I'd like to ride the Blue Ridge Parkway and do the Foothills Trail as well."

Jeff says, "I like working on the trail and working with people. I spend about eight to ten hours a week on MST work now. When I was president of FMST, I was spending more time on the MST than on my work. I'll always be doing something on the MST. With Kate Dixon, our executive director, the MST is in good hands."

# Chapter 4
# The Coastal Plains

## Route from Falls of the Neuse to the Cedar Island Ferry–250 miles

The MST in the Coastal Plains moves out of the Triangle (Raleigh, Durham and Chapel Hill), passing farms, roadside cemeteries and tiny towns. Here the trail is almost completely on back roads until you board the ferry to Cedar Island. The pine warbler, the signature bird for this portion of the MST, is common in pine forests of the Coastal Plains. Red-winged blackbirds flash their colors around brackish marshes and wet grasses.

The road from Falls of the Neuse in Wake Forest is narrow, twisty and very busy, but the traffic doesn't last long. Soon the trail is in the pastoral suburbs, passing gated communities mixed in with small home businesses.

You'll walk through the center of Youngsville (population 650), past a coffee shop. It will be a long time before you have another opportunity to sit with a cup of coffee. In rural Franklin County, an old gas station advertises leaded gasoline for thirty cents per gallon, a leftover from the 1960s. Hill Ridge Farm, a recreational farm, offers hayrides, train rides and a playground for birthday parties or an afternoon of fun for young children. However, the barnyard animals are safely tucked away behind two fences. Is it for the protection of children or the goats and sheep?

The route takes you close to Zebulon, the big town here with 4,600 people, but basically heads down to Wilson. As the trail moves farther away from the Triangle, wetlands begin to appear. You'll pass tobacco and cotton fields. Swamps are more prevalent, and so are cemeteries. On Lamm Road in Wilson, the trail passes James B. Hunt High School. Jim Hunt, a former governor of North Carolina, came from Wilson, and his administration made education a priority. The Mountains-to-Sea Trail was conceived during Hunt's first term as governor.

Wilson is in the heart of North Carolina's historic tobacco country. From the outskirts of town, the trail goes through the small town of Black Creek and then Eureka, with a diner that seems busy only at breakfast time.

After skirting Goldsboro, the trail leads to downtown La Grange, which looks prosperous. Close to Kinston, the trail follows Old U.S. 70 through Dover and Cove City. The MST goes right through New Bern, home of Tryon Palace, the first capital of North Carolina.

Once over the Neuse River, you'll walk on busy NC 55 for a few miles. The trail turns toward the towns of Arapahoe and Minnesott, where a ferry leads to the Neusiok Trail in Croatan National Forest. After twenty-two miles in the forest, the trail comes out at Oyster Point. It's a good name since people in the tiny communities harvest oysters for themselves and for sale to local restaurants.

The trail crosses several inlets on bridges over the Atlantic Intercoastal Waterway. U.S. 70 leads to NC 12 through Cedar Island National Wildlife Refuge. Cedar Island Variety Store is the last chance for tourists to pick up supplies before they take the ferry to Ocracoke Island. It won't be easy to get this section of the MST off the road and into the woods.

## In Praise of Walking the Road

When Allen de Hart created the road route, he didn't start with a blank slate and say, "Where should the trail go?" He used the North Carolina bike routes as a starting point. The state had already identified quiet and scenic back roads for cycling. That was true in the Piedmont as well, but it becomes more obvious on this stretch, where there's almost no public land. In the Coastal Plains, the MST has been on the road since its inception. Friends of the MST is looking to make use of future greenways to get the trail off the road. But walking through tiny towns and meeting locals is one of the pleasures of the MST. A Lenoir County man learned that his house was on the path of the MST when a long-distance biker on the trail broke down in front of his house. In the spirit of true southern hospitality, he and his wife invited her to stay over until she could get her bike repaired.

The decision of how far to walk each day is probably most difficult in the Coastal Plains. Flat road walking is easy and seductive. You feel that you can just keep going and going. If you think about your general fitness and strength, you most certainly can. However, don't forget about your feet. They bear the brunt of the miles. Walking fifteen to seventeen or more miles a day on pavement, day after day, is tough on your feet.

The road skirts fields of various sizes, but size is relative; these fields are small compared to those in the Midwest. Some are in winter crop, others freshly plowed or ready for picking, depending on the season. Many fields also incorporate family cemeteries. Ancestors lie on the high point of the field under a lone oak tree. Other family members are buried right on the side of the road. It looks like the road may have split the property, but the cemetery is only on one side. Maybe this way people can drive and park right next to their departed kin.

On this section, dogs are under control. Some are chained or fenced, but others just seem to know that they shouldn't go past their property lines. They've been well trained. Every house has a polka-dot mailbox with a matching polka-dot flag. You really have to be house proud to live in a rural area like this. Residents must spend a lot of time on their houses and gardens. Camellias are in bloom on a March day. In North Carolina, red camellias pop out between glossy leaves when almost all other plants are still dormant. Nothing says the South like a camellia plant in the front garden.

The trail enters Black Creek, established 1779, with a population of 714, and follows its main street. In 1839, the first train ran through Black Creek, part of the route from Wilmington on the coast to Rocky Mount. The railroad came through the middle of town, bisecting the main street. There's a small grocery store, a police station and a beauty shop with a lonely owner sitting outside with her dog. The route goes past a huge cemetery. The town park is a welcome break from the road and sun.

## GROWING TOBACCO AND COTTON IN EASTERN NORTH CAROLINA

The MST goes through the heart of North Carolina tobacco and cotton country. The best place to learn about tobacco is the Tobacco Farm Life

Museum in Kenly, close to Wilson. If you visit on a cool weekday, you might be the only person in the museum. Melody Worthington, the curator, is eager to answer questions.

North Carolina is still the largest producer of tobacco in the United States. The noxious weed, as tobacco was called, is native to the Western Hemisphere. Indians smoked, chewed and drank tobacco since 1000 BC. Tobacco delayed the struggle for American independence and strengthened the Loyalist cause. Today it's grown mainly in the Southeast.

After the Civil War ended the reign of King Cotton, growing tobacco became more popular and is credited for rebuilding the state. There are two types of tobacco crops in North Carolina. Flue tobacco, grown here in the Coastal Plains for cigarettes, is heat cured. It's called flue tobacco because the curing process uses flues or ducts to convey heat inside the tobacco barn. Charcoal is burned instead of wood. Burley tobacco, used for cigars, is grown in the Western North Carolina mountains, where it's air-cured.

Melody suggests watching a film produced on the Holland Farm before starting to tour the museum. Paul and Jean Holland take people through each step of the tobacco process. It's a serious movie, but as they say at the beginning, they are not encouraging anyone to smoke.

Even today, growing tobacco is very labor-intensive. In mid-February, farmers start tobacco plants in trays floating in water to speed up the germination process. They even mow the plants indoors. The Hollands use a three-year rotation cycle of tobacco, soy and cotton. By the end of April, they're ready to transplant the young shoots outdoors.

Tobacco plants are separated by hand and dropped mechanically in the soil. Lots of fertilizer, disinfectants and insecticide are applied. Farmhands cultivate the soil and look for bug worms. Since tobacco is grown for the leaves, not seeds, the flowers are topped off by hand. Too bad, because the pink trumpet-shaped flowers at the top of the plant are very attractive.

First, the workers harvest the bottom leaves called lugs. They then collect mid-range leaves and then the top leaves that produce the best tobacco. Each picking goes through the same processing. Tobacco is heat-cured for seven days, then baled in large cubes and taken to market. The film emphasizes again that growing tobacco is very labor-intensive. The *great* migrant worker accommodations are displayed. Farmhands stay in a large metal building with only a couple of windows.

Traditionally, tobacco was sold at auctions. Farmers went into town with their tobacco bundles and hoped to get a price that at least covered their costs. A museum exhibit shows a video of a tobacco auction. The auctioneer spews out fast gibberish, but his audience understands him. With the auction system, farmers were paid once a year, which must have required some serious financial management. The money they made was mostly spent on paying off their debts, and there wasn't much left over for the rest of the year. Now most tobacco farmers contract directly with a tobacco company and get paid regularly.

The museum is spreading out from just tobacco to the farm life that tobacco sustained. Tobacco is notorious for depleting and eroding the soil. Traditionally, settlers moved on when soil was too poor to continue farming. However, by the 1920s, you couldn't do that anymore because there was no place to move. Hugh Hammond Bennett, a North Carolinian, studied soil erosion and worked for the Bureau of Soils starting in the early 1900s. He encouraged crop rotation and planting cover crops. He's now considered the father of soil conservation.

Outside the museum building, the Brown family home shows how people lived in the early 1900s. The wood-framed house was left empty in 1960 and later donated to the museum. With furniture and curtains, the house looks very comfortable, even for today. The Browns appear to have lived a lot better than the Woodies in the Cataloochee area of Great Smoky Mountains National Park at the same time. Here, the dining room and kitchen are in a separate building from the main house. A smokehouse, outhouse and a tobacco barn with tobacco still in the building are scattered around the main dwelling. Each building has a sign that reads, "Thank you for not smoking."

Elisa New discusses tobacco as a source of progress in *Jacob's Cane*, her family history that spans from Eastern Europe to Baltimore. Between the Civil War and World War I, no product better exemplified the struggle and gains made for social progress than tobacco. But there was a large difference between how Europeans and Americans used tobacco. Europeans created devices for the enjoyment of tobacco, such as pouches, boxes, cigarette holders and even polite literature expressing the charms of tobacco. The author contends that in the United States, tobacco use was crude. Smoke stained cabin walls, and men chewed and spit tobacco juice, not always in a spittoon.

After the introduction of rolling machines, cigarettes could be manufactured without expensive craft labor. Mass production of cigarettes helped to create the Duke family fortune in Durham. Cigarettes attracted an urban population that didn't want to chew or smoke a pipe. But in much of the South, men and even some women still shunned cigarettes as sissy-like.

Another farm life exhibit explains that in eastern North Carolina, the custom of burying kin on private property dates back to European settlers. The MST passes many private grave sites on the roadside. Some graves are in the middle of a field on a high point under a large pine tree, but most lie on the side of the road, where presumably you can step out of your car and be with your loved one. Gravestones are engraved suitably with names and dates. Unlike the mountains, rock stumps aren't used to mark grave sites. Even today, locals want to be buried on land they were emotionally connected to and near family members they left behind. Private cemeteries can be personalized to the taste of the family, with plants, benches and statues. Private grave sites are also cheaper than church properties, which charge for upkeep in their cemeteries. Best of all, there are no rules to follow. However, it's becoming more difficult to get a permit to bury relatives on private land.

Cotton is still grown in eastern North Carolina. It may no longer be king, but it is a way of life and a living. These fields look small, barely worth bothering with, but it turns out that cotton is still an important crop. The United States is a large cotton grower, along with China and India. Most southern states grow cotton, and we export much of the cotton we grow.

In winter, cotton fields still hang on to dead stalks waiting to be plowed under. White wisps dangle from the stems. Cotton floats around the fields like dandelion angels. We imagine cotton growing as it was in the last two centuries. It factored in the perpetuation of slavery in the South, the Civil War and, later, much of the sharecropping system. In the Sally Field movie *Places in the Heart*, set in the Depression, poor farmhands picked cotton by hand in the burning sun. The backbreaking work gave rise to the expression "cotton-picking," with the last "g" usually missing. After World War II, mechanical harvesters made harvesting cotton much easier.

As you zip down a back road at fifty-five miles an hour, you can't tell cotton from soybeans. You have to see it close up in a field. The cotton flower is a cone with layers of attractive pink and white petals. Once mature, cotton is held in round pods called bolls. When the boll breaks open and you feel the soft white ball, there's no question that you're in a cotton field. Trying to pull the seeds out of the cotton by hand takes forever, and half of the cotton goes with it. That's why the invention of the cotton gin by Eli Whitney was such a turning point in the history of cotton and, ultimately, the United States.

Cotton in eastern North Carolina is planted in early May and harvested in October. About a week before they're going to pick the cotton, farmers spray their fields to encourage defoliation. There's little organic cotton grown anywhere. The leaves drop off and aren't gathered along with the bolls. Once harvested, the cotton is compressed in large modules and left in the field until it's ready for ginning ("gin" was short for "engine").

The gin house—no connection with booze—is a large building full of machinery that takes cotton through many processes. First, the cotton has to be dry. Cotton is heated slightly to make it easier to separate and remove the leaves and twigs trapped in the white balls. After the cotton is completely cleaned of trash and seeds, 1,200 pounds in the field reduces to 500 pounds of clean cotton. Cottonseed becomes a component of cattle feed or made into oil.

In the early 1990s, farmers started growing more cotton or switched from corn to cotton because the price shot up. Now the price has come down. "Farming is like gambling," a gin house manager says as he checks the price of cotton on his smartphone.

We send our cotton overseas in five-hundred-pound bales. They spin it, weave it and make clothing out of the material, only to ship the finished goods back to the United States. Does that make us a third-world country?

## KATHY KYLE:
### REMEMBERING A COASTAL PLAINS CHILDHOOD

Kathy Kyle remembers growing up in the Coastal Plains in the 1970s. "I'm not a southerner, though I spent most of my life in the South. My family is from Missouri. So I consider myself a midwesterner."

Kathy was born in Independence, Missouri, but moved with her family to Goldsboro in 1969 when she was seven years old. Her father, Ken Kyle, became the city manager of Goldsboro, and the family lived there until Kathy finished the tenth grade.

"In the Goldsboro school system, white kids were in the minority. Black teachers were the best, but the overall quality of the school wasn't good. Goldsboro was too small for segregated schools. Parents who wanted their children to go to a white school enrolled them to either a county school or private school." Kathy recalls that "the neighborhoods were segregated, and there was no socialization outside of school between white and black kids."

Kathy and her siblings enjoyed a small-town idyllic childhood that inner-city children can only dream about. Tobacco barns and horse stables were very common in their area. They lived on the outskirts of town surrounded by fields and woods, so they played outside a lot. The siblings shared a palomino, Ramus. Only Stony Creek separated them from Seymour Johnson Air Force Base. Kathy's nine-year-old brother, John, found a napalm bomb in the woods behind their house. He told their mother, who contacted the air force base. John took them on a short hike to show the bomb to the airmen, and they removed it.

"It makes you wonder how many other bombs there were around there," Kathy says. "John liked to dress in camouflage when he was a child, but that didn't inspire him to join the military." Goldsboro annexed the air force base while Ken Kyle, her father, was city manager. That was quite an accomplishment since it brought in extra tax revenues to the city.

"We moved to Goldsboro from upper New York State. I always felt like an outsider. Goldsboro almost seemed like a third-world country then. People in the town owned land and passed down lots of family tradition. They fished and hunted but didn't mingle with others," Kathy said. Her parents were considered outsiders as well. Her father didn't fish or hunt. Her mother was active with the arts council and took art and design courses in Raleigh.

At the end of Kathy's sophomore year, the family moved back to Overland Park, a suburb of Kansas City. "I went to Shawnee Mission High School, which was very different from Goldsboro," Kathy remembers. "My new school had an indoor swimming pool and kids drove Corvettes. It was an upscale school, and I had a hard time catching up academically after Goldsboro. On the other hand, my older brothers had found Goldsboro High so easy that they felt they were done with school."

In 1961, at the height of the Cold War, two hydrogen bombs fell in nearby Faro, a tiny village close to the MST. Because no explosion occurred, this potential tragedy never made it into the history books. A B-52 bomber crashed, and three of the eight crew members died. One bomb parachuted with little damage, but the other is still buried in a boggy field full of quicksand. Since it contained uranium, the air force was concerned. It bought an easement so no one can dig on the site where the bomb fell. The state still conducts yearly testing of the groundwater.

In the Coastal Plains, the MST goes into tiny communities. But a trail town can be off the trail, if it has the right services. Could Goldsboro be an MST trail town? Today Goldsboro is a large city of thirty-eight thousand people. Its wide downtown streets are quiet with many vacant stores. The Paramount Theater will be the leading edge of revival in the city center. Built in 1882 as an office building, the Paramount was a movie theater until it closed in the 1980s. Now it's been renovated as a venue for live theater.

Temple Oheb Shalom, opened in 1886, was the second-oldest Jewish synagogue in North Carolina, but the building is now a soup kitchen. A sculpture of a pig guards the front entrance of the kitchen. "The building is well taken care of," says a kitchen worker. They're doing good work in a blighted neighborhood. Goldsboro is probably too large and too spread out to be a good trail town.

## SMITHFIELD, A TRAIL TOWN?

In an attempt to get the MST off the road in the Coastal Plains, the trail may shift to a route that goes from Clayton to Smithfield on the western side of Goldsboro. There are plans to build a greenway along the Neuse River. Almost three miles of Buffalo Creek Greenway, which goes from downtown Smithfield to the Community Park, are already in place. Buffalo Creek Greenway on the Neuse River includes the spot that gave the town its name. In 1759, John Smith, one of the area's earliest settlers, petitioned to operate a ferry where the Neuse River cut through his property. The site became known as Smith's Ferry. His son, John Jr., built a house on a rise overlooking the river and the ferry. The building was turned into an inn, providing overnight accommodations for travelers, and reverted to a private house, which is still standing. Bikers, walkers, joggers and even an occasional angler enjoy the greenway.

Smithfield, population about twelve thousand, is the county seat of Johnston County. The small downtown area on the Neuse River is lively with jewelry stores, financial services companies, a photographic equipment shop and even a three-dollar movie theater. Several bail bondsmen's offices occupy storefronts, but that's what you would expect around the courthouse.

Orchard House Booksellers also serves as a downtown coffeehouse. This independent bookstore survives by specializing in music events and drug and alcohol recovery books. The friendly atmosphere invites visitors to meet residents and residents to connect with one another. The Johnston County Heritage Center, housed in the original site of the First Citizen Bank building, serves as the local museum. The bank donated the building to the county when it moved to Raleigh. The large steel vault is kept open for visitors.

"There's no more room in Raleigh, so people are moving here," a museum volunteer said. "Smithfield is one of the fastest-growing places in the state." It's only thirty miles southeast of Raleigh, and housing is probably much cheaper, at least for now.

The Ava Gardner Museum is on the next block. Ava Gardner grew up on a tobacco farm close to Smithfield and became a glamorous movie star. She was considered one of the most beautiful women of her time. She starred in many popular movies in the 1950s through the 1970s and played opposite the major leading men of her day, including Richard Burton, Clark Gable, Burt Lancaster and Gregory Peck. Her marriages and relationships were as sensational and famous as her movie roles. Her longest marriage of nine years was to Frank Sinatra.

But who would think of creating an Ava Gardner museum? Tom Banks is a major fan who lived in the area. From the time Ava planted a kiss on Tom's cheek when he was twelve years old, Banks was smitten. No matter where he and his wife found themselves, they collected Ava's clippings, posters, photographs and anything else they could find about her. Banks started a museum in 1982 and moved it around the area. The museum finally settled on Market Street in an abandoned Belk Department Store.

Smithfield sits close to the intersection of I-95 and U.S. 70. Here, these two roads use the railroad route that made this area flourish. Railroads transported first cotton and then tobacco to new markets. Southern Railway, built in 1854 by Atlantic and East Carolina Railway, was where U.S. 70 is now located. With train travel, a new world opened to Smithfield residents. According to Thomas J. Lassiter, author of *A Short History of Johnston County: 1746–1890*, before railroad service came to Johnston County, a one-way ticket by stagecoach from Goldsboro to Charlotte cost twenty-three dollars, which was more than the monthly income of a schoolteacher in the 1850s. The original train fare for the same trip was only five dollars.

The Wilmington and Weldon Line, built by the Atlantic Coast Railroad, came in 1886. As the principal artery of the Atlantic Coast, it stretched from Virginia to Florida. At the time, railroads offered prosperity that the Neuse River could never have delivered. Now, passenger rail is gone and I-95 brings in traffic on the same route.

This same prosperity will make Smithfield a fine trail town because it offers all the services that long-distance MST hikers might need. U.S. 70 Business has fast-food restaurants, a laundromat and plenty of motels. And farther back from downtown lies the reason that Smithfield is doing so well. It's the home of Carolina Premium Outlets, with eighty brand-name stores that stay open until 9:00 p.m., long after downtown Smithfield closes. MST hikers are not going to be interested in the Kitchen Store or Talbot clothes, but they'll enjoy the services that have come in because of the outlet mall.

Edmundson Cemetery in Greene County, one of the largest roadside cemeteries on the MST.

The MST has long passed the halfway point. Rhododendrons and mountain laurels disappeared awhile back. Loblolly pines and some long-leaf pines have replaced hemlock trees. There's no elevation for clear rushing streams. As the trail approaches the coast, the land becomes swampy. The water is still and brown, the color of tea without milk.

The swamps have been drained by building canals along the side of the road. A large strip of grass between the canal and the road creates a comfortable walking path. The trail leaves Wayne County and enters Greene County, where there are few churches but many family cemeteries. The Edmundson Cemetery, with its large crosses, sits on a road bend. James Edmundson, a lieutenant in the Revolutionary War who died in 1799, has the oldest readable grave. The Edmundsons are still in the area, some raising Butterball turkeys for your Thanksgiving dinner.

## LA GRANGE, A HAPPY PLACE

Just walking the length of La Grange's main street, you can feel that the town is a good place to live. La Grange, between Goldsboro and Kinston in Lenoir County, has fewer than three thousand people. Small, well-maintained houses built in the early 1900s line the main street. Residents sit on their large porches in colorful rocking chairs waiting to chat with walkers. Without a coffee shop on the main street, old men congregate in front of an electrical supply store, their version of the Chatterbox Café in *Lake Wobegon*. The best place to get a cup of coffee is at the Hess station, which doubles as a Dunkin' Donuts shop. The coffee is quite good, and you can sit on a stoop around the side of the building.

La Grange was first named Moseley Hall after Matthew Moseley, a captain in the Virginia militia during the Revolutionary War who settled in the area in 1777. It was the birthplace of William Dunn Moseley, the first governor of Florida. According to *La Grange—the Garden Spot Continues to Bloom* by Patsy M. Boyette, the Norfolk and Southern Railroad Company completed the railroad through Moseley Hall in 1858. The railroad brought goods and people, which boosted the settlement's growth. However, it also brought the Civil War closer to the area. The town served as a supply and arsenal headquarters during the war.

After the Civil War, the town wanted to incorporate. It needed a fresh start and a new name. It chose *La Grange* after Marquis de Lafayette's estate near Paris. General Lafayette served as a Continental army volunteer during the Revolutionary War. *Grange* means "barn" in French, not a particularly glamorous name. Maybe remembering a previous victory in the Revolutionary War just felt right.

After going over U.S. 70, the trail turns on Jenny Lind Road, named after a popular nineteenth-century Swedish opera singer. You'll cross the Neuse River and pass by a large swamp filled with bald cypress. Now you can really feel like you're in the Coastal Plains. Nothing says swamp like cypress trees.

According to David Blevins and Michael P. Schafale in *Wild North Carolina*, cypress trees are related to sequoias and redwoods. These trees can live over one thousand years, and North Carolina has the oldest stand of cypress east of the Rockies. Cypress trees don't blow over because their roots hold firmly to the watery soil. If you've seen bald cypress, you've seen its knees. The wooden protrusions rise around the tree in a helter-skelter pattern. Some say that knees carry air to the roots since the trees are standing in water. Others think that they provide stability and protection against the trees blowing over.

It could be that knees evolved in response to past environmental conditions that no longer exist. Though there have been many theories about the purpose of cypress knees, they remain a mystery.

## NEW BERN, THE FIRST CAPITAL OF NORTH CAROLINA

MST hikers are eager to get to New Bern since it represents another landmark on their eastbound trek. New Bern is a charming city and the largest that the MST traverses. If you want to understand all those terms about the American Revolution that you half remember from school, New Bern is the place to do it.

The trail goes south of Kinston, then through Cove City and comes into New Bern via NC 55, a four-lane commercial road with fast-food restaurants, a laundromat, auto repair shops and the Craven County medical complex. New Bern is a good place to resupply and get ready for the rest of your MST trek. Soon the trail weaves into the historic area with megachurches, lovely homes and several bed-and-breakfasts.

Located at the confluence of the Neuse and the Trent Rivers, New Bern has almost thirty thousand people. The city, founded in 1710, celebrated its 300th anniversary by connecting with people from its old world counterpart in Bern, Switzerland.

John Lawson, a British traveler, explored the Carolinas in 1700 and left us with *A New Voyage to Carolina*. Lawson started a five-hundred-mile voyage into the Carolina backcountry with a group of Englishmen and Native Americans. From present-day Charleston, they traveled to Hillsborough west of Eno River State Park and back east in two months, ending up in the settlement of Bath on the Pamlico Sound. During the journey, Lawson kept a detailed journal, made sketches and maps and gathered specimens of plants and animals. When he went back to Europe, he convinced Baron Christoph von Graffenried from Bern to bring over Swiss and German settlers. *Bern*, in German, means "bear." Painted bear sculptures are sprinkled all over the city. Lawson was recently inducted into the North Carolina Literary Hall of Fame, about four hundred years after he published his travel memoirs. Talk about waiting patiently for literary recognition!

In *New Bern History 101*, local historian Edward Barnes Ellis Jr. writes that if John Lawson had not established New Bern and convinced Graffenried to bring his colonists, New Bern would have been a different place. The skilled artisans that came over from Europe didn't build crude log cabins like in Jamestown, Virginia. They started with plank-sided frame houses from the earliest days.

William Tryon, the royal governor of North Carolina, was not the first governor of North Carolina, but he left the biggest mark on New Bern. He made a recommendation to King George III that New Bern become the permanent capital of the Province of North Carolina. Tryon brought over John Hawks to design a fashionable house befitting a royal governor. Hawks designed the palace to resemble the fashionable Georgian houses of London. Tryon Palace, still the town's showcase, was completed in 1770. But Tryon and his family didn't stay long. After he and his family lived in the palace for only a year, he became royal governor of New York, probably considered a promotion.

When Josiah Martin was appointed royal governor of North Carolina, the rumblings of a revolt against England were getting louder. Martin filled the palace with expensive furniture. Rumors started that he was stockpiling weapons in the palace and was going to foment a slave rebellion. Martin and his family fled New Bern. After American independence, Tryon Palace became the first capital of the state of North Carolina. President Washington visited and danced in the palace in 1791. When the capital of North Carolina was moved to Raleigh in 1794, the palace turned into a school, then a boardinghouse and then a Masonic lodge. It burned four years later.

Rebuilding the palace has its own story. People in New Bern society thought about rebuilding Tryon Palace since the 1930s, but sometimes it takes one person with a dream—and some money. Maude Moore Latham lived in Greensboro but was a New Bern native. She often spoke of her hope that the palace might be reconstructed somehow. As a garden club member, she published *Old Homes and Gardens of North Carolina* in 1939. Fortuitously, in the same year, the North Carolina Society for the Preservation of Antiquities was organized. Around the same time, by another happy chance, New Bern activist Gertrude Carraway discovered the original palace drawings in the New York Historical Society Library.

In 1944, Latham established a trust fund dedicated to the rebuilding of the palace. She was a forward-thinking woman and realized that volunteers would not be able to maintain the new palace. Her trust fund required that the State of North Carolina purchase the land and maintain the site after it was restored. Latham became the first chair of the Tryon Palace Commission. A 1945 picture of the original commission members shows a group of women of indeterminate age wearing somber dresses, hats and gloves. Several men are also in the photograph in suits and ties.

After Latham's death in 1951, and with skilled financial management from her son-in-law, enough money had been put aside to pay for the reconstruction of the palace. The house needed mid-eighteenth-century furniture and historically accurate gardens. Later, Latham's daughter, May Gordon Kellenberger, followed in her mother's footsteps to become chair of the Tryon Palace Commission. She worked on the restoration while her husband oversaw the trust. An army of professionals was hired to re-create as authentic a palace as possible. A long time had elapsed since 1798 when the palace burned. It's easy to forget that people had built houses and lived on the site. During the early days of restoration, the commission bought individual parcels of land one by one and removed their buildings.

The restored palace also needed proper furniture and effects. When William Tryon moved from New Bern to become governor of New York, he took all his furnishings with him. Later, his New York mansion burned, and everything was destroyed, but he was able to list all his losses, room by room. The Brits were always good with paperwork. In 1952, in what the booklet *Tryon Palace: Its Restoration and Preservation* by the Tryon Palace Commission calls "almost miraculously," an inventory of Governor Tryon's possessions was found in Great Britain. This became a guide for buying furniture of similar type. Kellenberger and her colleagues went on furniture shopping trips in Scotland and England.

By 1957, the director had started training hostesses to interpret the palace for the public. Some attended a short course on historic housekeeping because cleaning a historic palace is not the same as cleaning a modern house. Landscape architects designed sixteen acres of gardens inspired by eighteenth-century British estates. Kitchen gardens, wilderness gardens and formal gardens with statues each have their distinctive feel. Completed at a cost of $3.5 million, the palace opened in 1959 and is now under the direction of the North Carolina Division of Cultural Resources.

Visiting Tryon Palace today is a delightful experience. Present-day docents are enthusiastic and knowledgeable. The women wear long flowered dresses and white cloth caps on their heads. On many weekends, the Tryon Palace Fife and Drum Corp march around the grounds, playing colonial military music. Sometimes the teenager and adult band members dress in a uniform with navy knickers and vests, tricorn hats and long white socks that meet their trousers. Other times they're in casual clothes, with fife and drum T-shirts.

Decorated fiberglass bears stand all over New Bern.

Several streets of restaurants, galleries and gift shops are a short walk from the palace. Whimsical bear sculptures are scattered all through the downtown. At the corner of Middle and Pollock Streets, Caleb Bradham, a pharmacist, created a soft drink to serve at his soda fountain. First known as Brad's Drink, the beverage was a mixture of carbonated water, sugar, pepsin, kola nut extract and vanilla. By 1898, he called his drink Pepsi-Cola. Later, Bradham mixed and packaged his syrups in the back of the drugstore. Bottling was the next step, and the drink was very popular for many years. Customers expected to pay only five cents a bottle.

During World War I, Bradham invested heavily in sugar to ensure a steady supply at a known price. When the sugar market plummeted, so did his business. By 1923, his Pepsi-Cola company was bankrupt, and he sold what was left of his company. The buyers reformulated the drink and made it a success. Today, the original store holds a wealth of Pepsi merchandise, from bibs to belt buckles. It's a fun place to visit.

As of this writing, New Bern's most famous resident is probably the novelist Nicholas Sparks, best known for *The Notebook* and *Nights in Rodanthe*. Many of his books were made into movies. Sparks did not grow up in New Bern. With his means, he could live anywhere, which speaks well of the area.

## To the Minnesott Ferry

After New Bern, the MST crosses the Neuse River on a busy bridge on U.S. 17. Hiking on a six-lane bridge without a pedestrian walkway is a daunting proposition. You can walk it and hope that cars don't stray on the narrow shoulder. You can hitchhike, or you can follow Jerry Ellis's example. Ellis, a Cherokee, walked the Trail of Tears route from Tahlequah, Oklahoma, back home to Fort Payne, Alabama, and wrote *Walking the Trail: One Man's Journey Along the Cherokee Trail of Tears*. On his nine-hundred-mile trek, much of it on roads, Ellis needed to cross the Mississippi River on a bridge without a walkway. He felt that walking across the bridge was dangerous, but he didn't want to stick his thumb out. So he came up with the brilliant idea to call the local police station and ask for an escort. He expected a brush-off, but to his amazement, the officer said, "Sure. What time do you want to cross?" The next morning, a TV crew, along with the police, greeted Ellis. He walked in front of a cop on a motorcycle with its red light twirling. Traffic backed up behind the parade, and Ellis felt he had to run with a fifty-pound pack on his back. Maybe the New Bern police would be as cooperative, but only if you asked them.

Once off the bridge, the trail continues on NC 55, a busy four-lane road with wide grassy verges. It turns on Neuse Road, passing large tree farms owned by Weyerhauser and crossing swampy areas. The area is poor, rural and isolated. An occasional car passes. A hawk is perched in the trees, and a bald eagle flies overhead. The trail leads through the town of Arapahoe, population 434. The name may sound Polynesian, but it's an Indian name from the Great Plains of Colorado and Wyoming. Arapahoe was founded a few years after New Bern by settlers leaving the New Bern colony.

In 1886, Bob Hardison and his friend Bob Bowden applied to the U.S. Postal Service for a post office to be located at "Bethany Crossroads" in Pamlico County. When the application was returned to them it was addressed to "Bob's Town," since there was already a "Bethany Crossroads" near Fayetteville. Neither Bob liked "Bob's Town," so they came up with a different name—Arapahoe, named after one of the Bobs' horses.

Today, Arapahoe has a supermarket and several churches. It closed the traditional school and replaced it with a charter school in a smaller building. The community of Arapahoe flows right into Minnesott Beach, the last town before the ferry. Minnesott Beach is located at the site of an old Indian settlement, which may have been one of the largest Indian trading centers in the South Atlantic states.

The Minnesott Ferry crosses the Neuse River.

The city leaders recognize that their time has passed. Their website explains, "Back in the 1930s through 1950s, in our heyday, we were a thriving vacation destination. Today we have settled into a quiet golfing, sailing, and retirement community which offers an 18-hole golf course, marina, and world class boys' camp."

The Minnesott Ferry at the end of the road is still free. The crossing of the Neuse River takes twenty minutes.

## BACKPACKING THE NEUSIOK TRAIL

You're back to backpacking, if only for a short distance, in Croatan National Forest, one of four national forests in North Carolina. After miles of road walking, you'll enter Havelock and follow the Neusiok Trail in the southeastern corner of the forest. If you've chosen to bike the road, you'll need to dispose of your bike somehow and put on a backpack.

Croatan is almost completely surrounded by four rivers. The Neusiok Trail, named for an early local Indian tribe, is pronounced New-see-ock.

It extends from the Neuse River to the Newport River. There's not much written about the trail, and various sources give it a different distance. The map says 26.0 miles, and a PDF file says 20.0. A recent GPS track came up with 22.1 miles—that's the correct mileage.

Croatan National Forest ain't the Smokies. Mountain hikers might think that the backpack is going to be a cakewalk because the trail is so flat. The terrain is swampy and, by April, already buggy. Croatan Forest has poisonous snakes, chiggers, mosquitoes and ticks. It's a jungle out here, but it will be a different experience.

The trail starts at Pine Cliffs Recreation Area, a couple of miles MST east of the Minnesott Ferry landing. Hikers tromp on sand, a far cry from the rocks and roots of the mountains. Even Falls Lake Recreation Area around Durham and Raleigh, the previous trail on the MST, had hard-packed soil. Even though you're walking by the Neuse River, the scenery is straight out of the South Pacific. The river is wide and looks more like an ocean inlet. If you ignore the trees on the other side of the river, you could be in Fiji.

But it doesn't sound very Pacific. Croatan is close to Cherry Point Marine Corps Air Station, a pilot training station. Jets fly overhead. You'll hear guns firing, though it's just target practice. The marine base opened in 1941, just before the attack on Pearl Harbor, while Croatan National Forest dates back to the mid-1930s. During World War II, no one cared that the military encroached on peaceful woods. At the entrance to the military base, a sign proclaims, "Pardon our noise, it's the sound of freedom."

If this landscape is unfamiliar to you, you'll want to walk slowly and stop to admire this strange scenery. Two ospreys fly around a huge nest built on a treetop. A kingfisher has planted itself on a branch to survey the river. You might find a box turtle, wild turkeys and a green anole, a tiny lizard. Crested-dwarf irises, a familiar flower in the mountains, have mixed in with swamp plants. Once off the beach, the trail goes past large bald cypress with their characteristic knees standing in tranquil brown water.

Copperhead Landing Shelter, 3.4 miles from the start, is the first of three shelters on the Neusiok Trail. Because of ticks, locals advise hikers to wear long pants and long-sleeved shirts. But it's going to be hot unless you're traveling through in the dead of winter.

The trail passes by pocosins, swamp bogs raised by the buildup of organic material. Pocosins are walls of scrawny trees, oddly shaped bushes and greenbrier vines that will attach to anything, including skin. Blevins and Schafale, in *Wild North Carolina*, describe walking through a pocosin as like wrestling a bear. This type of swamp occurs almost exclusively in North Carolina.

The Carteret County Wildlife Club designed and built the Neusiok Trail in 1971. The area is a swamp, but unless you want a real jungle experience, the trail needs boardwalks and bridges. One boardwalk is almost a mile long.

Terry Smith, president of Carteret County Wildlife Club and Friends of the MST board member, is a dedicated Neusiok Trail maintainer. "These boardwalks require almost constant maintenance," Terry says. "Boards have to be carried in, and they're not light." Floods, hurricanes and tree falls can obstruct the trail. You don't want to get lost here. In the mountains, you can climb to a view or remember a large boulder to reorient yourself. To a swamp newbie, the scenery all looks the same.

It's a green and brown world, punctuated by a clump of pink azaleas. Hikers walk in single file because the trail is narrow. If you're in front of the line, you'll be breaking up spider webs using hiking poles, your hands and sometimes your face. You might want to take turns leading, as if you were breaking trail in the snow. Words have been etched into several boardwalks—"In memory of"—but the most memorable is "Cotton Mouth Spa." After all the snake warnings, the most common snake might be a thin green one, nicknamed a shoelace snake.

Boardwalk on the Neusiok Trail.

This area was used for making moonshine, but you won't find stills or barrels along the trail. Today, geocaching paraphernalia is hidden in the woods. A metal box with several plastic knickknacks has been left for the next group, which will record their finds and add their own trinkets.

The Neusiok Trail moves into a pine savannah where longleaf pines tower over a groundcover of wiregrass. The trees have straight trunks without lower branches. True to their name, longleaf pine needles can reach a foot long, creating a soft carpet underfoot. The trees grow far apart to allow sunlight to reach the ground. After the dense swampy vegetation, it's a pleasure to walk through this section. Longleaf pines depend on fire so they can grow without competing with other trees close by. To keep the longleaf pine forest healthy, the Forest Service needs to burn the area regularly. Fire clears out the undergrowth and promotes seed germination. Burning also controls pests. However, while other vegetation will burn, longleaf pines can withstand most fires because of their thick bark and coating of resins. Wiregrass also benefits from fire, reemerging and flowering after a burn. The endangered red-cockaded woodpecker needs longleaf pines to survive and is supposed to nest in several areas in Croatan National Forest. This fussy bird will only excavate cavities in living pine trees.

During the era of sailing ships, before the Civil War, longleaf pines were responsible for the economic boom in coastal Carolina. Tar, pitch and turpentine, known as naval stores, were extracted from these pines to keep ships sailing across the Atlantic. Tar, used to waterproof ship riggings, is removed by slowly burning dead pine wood in a kiln. However, making turpentine involves cutting into a live tree to get the resin to run, which is not healthy for pine trees. Turpentine was used for fuel, as an antiseptic for wounds, for cleaning carpets and removing stains. It was the all-purpose WD-40 of its day.

For a time, coastal North Carolina supplied a quarter of the world's naval stores. This is where you get the expression "tar heel," the nickname for a North Carolinian. Pine trees stood as far as the eye could see. If you walked barefoot through longleaf pine trees, some tar was bound to stick to your feet. The expression was used extensively in the Civil War, and the name stuck. But for most people today, the Tar Heels is the UNC–Chapel Hill football team.

With the coming of steam engines, wooden ships disappeared and so did the need for tar and turpentine. *Harper's Weekly* published a telling drawing showing General Burnside's fleet coming into New Bern during the Civil War. About half the boats were sailing ships, and half were iron steamships.

When sailing ships disappeared, no one required products from longleaf pine trees. The Havelock region plunged into a depression that lasted until the marine base came to the area. The federal government took the few houses left on the property it wanted by eminent domain. But the cemeteries are still here, tended by military personnel.

Dogwood Camp Shelter is about ten miles from the start of the trail, close to Highway 101. Usually shelters are not built so close to roads, since they attract people who are more interested in partying than hiking, but it doesn't seem to be a problem here. About three adults can fit comfortably in these shelters. However, the standard advice from experienced local hikers is, "You don't want to sleep here. Too full of crawling insects." It's best to bring a tent.

The trail continues on a two-mile gravel road. Locals call it a turnpike, a trail lifted by using crushed marlstone, a natural mixture of clay and calcium with fossils so water can drain on both sides. You can stop and camp anywhere, but you'll only have the water you're carrying with you. After almost twenty miles, you'll reach Black Jack Lodge Shelter, close to Mill Creek Road. A decorated wooden sign with the name of the shelter

Sharon checks her feet at Black Jack Lodge Shelter after a long day on the Neusiok Trail.

hangs in the back. At each shelter, a notebook in a plastic bag is hooked on the shelter wall. Hikers sign their names and destinations and sometimes add a story, poem or drawing. Around the shelter, flattened tree stumps for seats encircle the campfire. The last tenants have left plastic jugs of brown water. You prime the pump by pouring water over the top of the pump to wet the old plastic mechanism. After the water soaks in, you start pumping. Lighter-colored water comes out of the pump. It is still advised to treat the water, but it's better than the brown liquid from swamps.

After that, it's only 2.5 miles to walk to Oyster Point, the end of the Neusiok Trail. The trail passes through a savannah, a sea of grass waving in the breeze. The altitude gain on the whole trail is only 250 feet. Many people in Western North Carolina have steeper driveways.

From here, it's about forty-five miles of walking to the Cedar Island ferry. The only altitude you'll encounter is when the trail crosses the Intercoastal Waterway several times on high bridges. This is oyster country. Several old buildings that used to process oysters and clams now stand empty. Divers have become independent operators. They dive for shellfish and sell to wholesalers, who then supply local restaurants. Each operator has marked his territory, and someone else had better not mess with it.

Crossing Core Creek Bridge on the Intercoastal Waterway.

Davis Shore Provisions is a must stop for MST hikers in an area where coffee shops are at a premium. The Davis store dates back to the early 1950s when Johnny Davis owned it, but that store closed years ago. Now it's a modern rendition of a general store with great coffee, ice cream and gifts. The key lime pie is amazingly good. The owners know they're located on the MST route and are very friendly to long-distance hikers.

## CEDAR ISLAND NATIONAL WILDLIFE REFUGE: PROTECTING WILDLIFE

The trail leaves the tiny communities and goes through Cedar Island National Wildlife Refuge. President Theodore Roosevelt authorized the first National Wildlife Refuge in 1903. Refuges manage land and water for animals and don't focus on recreation. As the U.S. Fish and Wildlife Service explains, "Parks are for people; refuges are for wildlife." There are no marked trails, but visitors can hunt, fish and bird, which the Fish and Wildlife Service calls "wildlife dependent recreational use."

This fifteen-thousand-acre refuge was created to protect the wintering habitat for thousands of migratory birds. Brackish marshes are home to a large number of ducks, shore birds and fish. Deer and bear live in the pocosins and woodlands, but hikers on NC 12 would be very lucky to see any large animals from the road. The Fish and Wildlife Service purchased the first portion of the island in 1964 and more in 1967. In 1970, an abandoned navy radar station dating from the Cuban Missile Crisis was obtained and converted into the refuge field office.

The refuge is managed by one employee, Kevin Keeler. He greets visitors, mows the lawn, patrols the road and answers the phone. Because of all his responsibilities, he's hard to catch in the office. Kevin is a one-person "chamber of commerce" and adds a human face to the refuge.

# Chapter 5

# The Outer Banks

## Route from Cedar Island Ferry to Jockey's Ridge State Park—83 miles

The ferry ride from Cedar Island to Ocracoke Island signals the beginning of the end of the MST walk. From here to Nags Head, the Outer Banks is quiet. Even today, in tourist terms, the area is considered out of the way with few services. The beach is almost deserted.

It doesn't take long to walk through the town of Ocracoke, and soon you're on the beach at Cape Hatteras National Seashore. Sanderlings run back and forth on the beach like wind-up toys.

The next ferry takes you to the town of Hatteras. NC 12 is the only road going north through the seashore. If you follow Scot Ward's directions, you'll walk on the beach for a while and then back on the road through another town, but you may choose to stick to the beach. Every town has its own character. Buxton is a busy place, at least compared to other towns on Cape Hatteras, though its permanent winter population is only 1,400 people.

You'll detour to climb Cape Hatteras Lighthouse, and then it's back on the beach. Avon, a charming town with a great coffee shop, is a good reason to move to the road. Hiking twelve to fifteen miles on the beach is different from a lazy thirty-minute walk between dips in the ocean. Here you need to be dressed for hiking, not for the beach, with a daypack and hiking poles. And lather on plenty of sunscreen as well because there's no shade.

The beach is marked off with ramps to allow off-road vehicles (ORVs) to drive to the water. Each ORV ramp is numbered, enabling hikers to keep track of their progress. The towns of Salvo, Waves and Rodanthe run together, and Rodanthe is the last place to get supplies before the end of your trek. Pea Island National Wildlife Refuge is almost thirteen miles of beach walking without a town alongside it. Because the refuge doesn't allow for off-road vehicles, you'll find almost no one on the beach. After the Bonner Bridge over Oregon Inlet, the trail goes inland to the Bodie Island Lighthouse. The Park Service is working on repairing the lighthouse, but for now, it's closed to visitors.

Hikers are shunted back to the beach for a few miles, but it's not far now to the end of the national seashore and into the town of Nags Head. The MST moves to the city streets and crosses U.S. 158, a busy highway, and into Jockey's Ridge State Park. The end of the trail has the tallest sand dunes on the Atlantic coast. With shifting sands, high winds, extreme temperatures and a lack of water, this park looks like a desert.

## Ocracoke Island: Lighthouse, Blackbeard and a British Cemetery

The ferry from Cedar Island to Ocracoke takes about two and a half hours. Because the North Carolina Department of Transportation runs the ferry system, the fees are very reasonable. A pedestrian can get on for one dollar and a car for fifteen dollars. You can only buy food from vending machines, so it's best to bring your own. Gulls, terns and pelicans following the ferry provide plenty of entertainment. Sometimes dolphins ride the waves.

After the ferry, you'll reach the first of several Cape Hatteras National Seashore Visitor Centers where you'll get information on the seashore and rules on beach closures. It's a fifteen-mile walk from ferry to ferry, so if you want to see the town of Ocracoke, you'll probably need to stay an extra day.

Ocracoke is a small, upper-crust island town, reached only by ferry, private plane or boat. The year-round population is eight hundred because winters can be chilly and quiet. In the summer, Ocracoke attracts visitors and summer residents with good restaurants, quality crafts and historic homes. Though the town is only a small part of the island, the streets don't feel crowded. The sights in town are definitely worth a few hours.

Three lighthouses were built on Cape Hatteras, each unique, which makes them easy to differentiate in photographs. The Ocracoke lighthouse, erected in 1823, is the second-oldest operating lighthouse in the country. It's painted all white and stands seventy-five feet high.

In a residential area of Ocracoke, the British government leased a small patch of land and used it as a cemetery. During World War II, German submarines attacked U.S. Navy boats. Great Britain offered to help and sent out twenty-four retrofitted trawlers to patrol shipping lanes off the coast of North Carolina. On May 11, 1942, a British ship, HMT *Bedfordshire*, was torpedoed and sunk by German U-boats. There were no survivors. Only four bodies were recovered and are now buried in Ocracoke. The small, neat graves with concrete gravestones are covered with pebbles and encircled by a white picket fence. Rupert Brooke's poem "The Soldier" comes to mind:

> *If I should die, think only this of me;*
> *That there's some corner of a foreign field*
> *That is for ever England.*

Brooke wrote about World War I, but the sentiment fits well here. Every year, the National Park Service, the U.S. Coast Guard and the British Royal Navy have a ceremony at the site, honoring the men who lost their lives in the attacks. A cemetery with a similar history lies farther up Cape Hatteras.

Many businesses in Ocracoke refer to Blackbeard, or Edward Teach, his real name. Blackbeard, along with his fellow pirates, roamed from the Caribbean to the Outer Banks and north to Virginia, robbing and plundering the ships they came across.

Blackbeard may have started as a loyal English subject in Queen Anne's War (1702–13), the second war in a series of French and Indian Wars. Contrary to its name, the French and Indian Wars were not between the French and the Indians but between France and England, with the Indians siding with the French. Blackbeard was a privateer, paid by the English government to plunder enemy ships. In this case, French vessels were the target.

However, when the war ended, Blackbeard and his loyal men continued to attack passing ships and crew. What had been patriotism became piracy. "After all," Blackbeard might say, "what is the difference between a privateer and a pirate? A piece of paper from the king."

Blackbeard renamed his ship *Queen Anne's Revenge* and was able to outfit it with three hundred men and forty cannons. He then sailed the Caribbean and the Atlantic along coastal waters of the American colonies, overwhelming merchant ships and stealing their cargo.

Even in the 1700s, Blackbeard knew about marketing. He branded himself as a violent pirate and looked the part. He was tall with a scraggly black beard, which gave him a fierce and menacing look. The flag on his ship added to his pirate image by depicting a heart dripping blood while a skeleton held an hourglass and spear.

The notorious pirate had created a nest at Ocracoke Inlet. At one point, Governor Charles Eden of colonial North Carolina promised to award citizenship to Blackbeard and his crew if they left their pirate days behind. Others say that Blackbeard bribed Governor Eden. Peace didn't last long, and Blackbeard was soon back to the excitement of pirating.

Frustrated coastal merchants and planters saw that Governor Eden didn't seem to have control of the colony and petitioned Governor Alexander Spotswood of Virginia to help restore peace. Governor Spotswood chose Lieutenant Robert Maynard of the British Navy to battle Blackbeard. Using two boats, Maynard chased and finally killed Blackbeard in late 1718 near Ocracoke. His head was cut off and mounted to Maynard's victorious ship, *Ranger*. After Blackbeard's death, his legend grew larger. A myth claims that Blackbeard's headless body swam three times around the ship. Governor Spotswood refused to return to England because he feared that Blackbeard's friends would intercept him at sea and avenge his death. When Blackbeard died, the golden age of piracy effectively came to an end in the area.

But what happened to all the treasure that Blackbeard was supposed to have looted? This remains a mystery and the source of many stories. Maynard was supposed to have found much of the pirates' booty stashed away in a barn owned by Governor Eden's secretary in Bath near the Pamlico River. More recently, in 1996, Blackbeard's boat, *Queen Anne's Revenge*, was discovered off the coast. Since then, divers have been bringing up artifacts, which are now permanently exhibited at the North Carolina Maritime Museum in Beaufort. Reclaiming artifacts is an expensive proposition, and the museum will be recovering relics for a long time.

After leaving town, the only accommodation is at the Ocracoke campsite, about a third of the way through the island. Once you start walking, you can go through town quickly, and soon you're finally on the beach. This is a major milestone on your MST trip. The National Park Service has protected the beach from development. There's just sand, waves and birds. Without a boardwalk, motels or snack bars, no one would confuse this beach with Coney Island. If you don't analyze what you see too closely, it looks like the beach has never been altered.

Get back on the road so as not to miss the Pony Pens. Ocracoke ponies ran free for centuries. Horses have been documented on Ocracoke since the first European settlers came to stay in the 1730s. There have been as many as three hundred horses on Ocracoke. Small and powerful, the Banker ponies, as they are known colloquially, are full-grown horses. Legend has it that the Banker horses of Ocracoke were left here by shipwrecked explorers in the sixteenth or seventeenth century. European ships commonly carried livestock to the New World. If a ship ran aground near the coast, animals were thrown overboard to lighten the load so the ship could be refloated. Sir Richard Grenville's ship *Tiger* hit bottom in Ocracoke in 1585, and his vessel may have unloaded Spanish mustangs on the island.

When Ocracoke was first settled, residents used ponies to pull carts for freight and fish and generally to make life easier on the island. The ponies helped the U.S. Lifesaving Service patrol beaches and haul equipment to shipwreck sites. In the late 1950s, Ocracoke Boy Scouts cared for the horses, becoming the only mounted scout troop in the nation. But when NC 12 was built through the Outer Banks in 1957 and the ponies had a few encounters with cars, the National Park Service penned them in and has watched over the remaining herd ever since. Currently, seventeen horses in the Ocracoke herd are kept in an enclosure and can be seen from the road.

After the horse pens, the tourists are gone and only birds remain on the beach. The wind has picked up. The white-capped waves roll in, and no one is swimming. Whatever gnats, mosquitoes and other bugs swarmed around you are now gone. Sanderlings chase retreating waves, and willets dig their long bills in the sand. A squadron of pelicans hovers over the water and then dives into the sea.

## PROTECTING BIRDS AND TURTLES

At some point, MST hikers will reach a beach closure; the area is off-limits to pedestrians and everything else. Walkers can't honestly say that they somehow missed a barrier. A rope is stretched across the sand from the dune to the water, and a large sign states that the beach is closed to protect birds. The seashore publishes a list of beach closures on the web for the week. Piping plovers, which are listed as threatened under the Endangered Species Act, and loggerhead turtles, which are proposed to be listed as threatened, can now nest in peace.

When you reach a beach closure, you can go back to the road or walk in the water. National park officials may not have thought about MST hikers when they created these regulations. They probably figured that if casual walkers see the closure signs, they'll just turn around and walk back, but that doesn't work for those trying to complete the MST. Eventually, when more people walk the MST, how long-distance hikers should negotiate beach closures will become a point of discussion.

At the end of Ocracoke Island, hikers take a forty-minute ferry to Hatteras Island. This ferry is free, creating some controversy. In an effort to balance the state budget, the North Carolina legislature is looking into charging for this ride. Ferry riders were surveyed to ask about their travel plans and how much they would be willing to pay. Tourists may accept a reasonable fare for an occasional visit to Ocracoke, but to locals, it's not that simple. Ferries are the only way on and off Ocracoke; they regard ferries as their road. However, others consider island living an expensive lifestyle choice. Their argument is that if people want to live in Ocracoke, let them pay the going rate.

## CLIMBING THE CAPE HATTERAS LIGHTHOUSE

Cape Hatteras National Seashore stretches over three islands, linked by ferries and NC 12, a narrow, two-lane road. The road goes through eight communities that are not technically part of the national seashore. MST hikers may find the road a welcome change from the beach and a little safer during a storm.

In the town of Hatteras, large houses face the road and back up to Pamlico Sound. Painted in peach, baby blue and sun yellow, the houses have balconies, porches and several outside staircases, some that seem to go nowhere and are just for show. Back on the beach, a solitary whimbrel feeds among a large number of sanderlings and willets. Whimbrels have long straight beaks that curve downward at the tip. But the MST is not on the beach for long. It goes through Frisco Campground and on a forest trail in Buxton Woods.

Open Ponds Trail, a 4.4-mile trail from the campground to the lighthouse, traverses through a maritime forest. Slogging through soft sand is not as easy as it sounds. Here your legs get good aerobic exercise. By getting off the beach, you'll see a new wildlife habitat.

Buxton Woods is the largest remaining maritime forest in North Carolina. Maritime forests hold soil in place and are the most stable part of the island. Live oaks and loblolly pines make up the canopy. The understory is a tangled web of grapevines and low bushes, such as wax myrtle and yaupon holly, a native shrub with thick leathery leaves. Yaupon was grown in the Tryon Palace gardens and used as a black tea, high in caffeine. In winter, birds also depend on the shiny red berries. All the vegetation needs to be able to withstand constant salt spray.

The trail is built through sand dunes and swales, low spots with freshwater ponds. Coming from the mountains, MST hikers can breeze through the flat trail, but there are plenty of challenges in the form of ticks, poison ivy and mosquitoes that thrive much of the year.

At the end of Open Ponds Trail, the MST passes a second British cemetery (the first was at Ocracoke). A white picket fence protects two graves that date back to World War II. Shells and rocks placed on top of the gravestones demonstrate that the departed have not been forgotten and that someone visited the grave sites. Early in 1942, the Germans knew that the United States was unprepared for war. Merchant ships traveling around the Florida panhandle and up the coast couldn't avoid the elbow of the North Carolina coast. The ships were very visible, and since blackout conditions were not yet enforced, there was plenty of light on land as well.

German U-boats prowling the waters around Cape Hatteras picked off these ships as easy targets, preventing the delivery of crude oil and food. In the first six months of 1942, almost four hundred ships were sunk. The area became known as "Torpedo Junction." The United States, with British help, was able to step up surveillance, and the attacks declined.

Finally, the MST arrives at the Cape Hatteras Lighthouse and Visitor Center. With its black-and-white stripes swirling upward like a huge barber pole, the lighthouse is an icon of the North Carolina coast. MST hikers have seen replicas of this lighthouse in people's front yards since the Piedmont. Cape Hatteras Lighthouse is the only one of the three at Cape Hatteras National Seashore that visitors can climb. You'll need to buy a ticket for a specific time. First, a ranger gives a short talk about the lighthouse. Mostly, she warns the group about the climb, which makes it sound like you'll be scaling Mount Everest. She echoes the website, which says:

*The climb is strenuous! The 248 iron spiral stairs to the top equal climbing a 12 story building. The stairs have a handrail only on one side and a landing every 31 steps. There is no air conditioning. It may be noisy, humid, hot and dim inside the lighthouse and there is two-way traffic on the narrow stairs.*

*Visitors with heart, respiratory or other medical conditions, or who have trouble climbing stairs, should use their own discretion as to whether to climb the tower.*

As an MST hiker, you'll be on top in five minutes. The 248 stairs and 165 feet of ascent is the most elevation on the MST since you've left the Piedmont. From the top, visitors can get a clear view of Diamond Shoals, a point where the Greenland current meets the Caribbean current. A series of sandy ridges and unpredictable weather make going around this elbow of land a hazardous venture. The Outer Banks are known as the "graveyard of the Atlantic" because many ships have sunk here. Still, boats found it convenient to use the Gulf Stream and favorable trade winds.

The original lighthouse was built in 1803 and fueled by whale oil. The current lighthouse, dating back from 1870, first used kerosene and was later electrified. The same pounding waves that cause ships so much trouble eroded the shoreline, moving the lighthouse closer to the ocean. The lighthouse was decommissioned and the signal moved to a steel tower. Twenty years later, the beach came back, and so did the beacon in the lighthouse. However, this was not a permanent solution.

In 1999, the National Park Service moved the lighthouse farther from the ocean, since it was about to get washed out to sea. The lighthouse now is 1,500 feet from the water, its original distance. The move took twenty-three days. Over twenty thousand visitors came to watch the daily progress. The visitor center shows a video on the complexity of the project. The Cape Hatteras Lighthouse still shines bright. The Coast Guard uses the lighthouse as a navigational aid and reference point.

The lighthouse is only part of the story. Lighthouse keepers and their families lived here until electricity came in. The current museum is in the Double Keeper's Quarters, a duplex house where two families lived. The principal keeper lived in his own house just next door. All the buildings were relocated when the lighthouse was moved.

Unaka Jennette, the last principal lighthouse keeper, and his wife, Sudie, raised seven children at the lighthouse. The Jennette family has been connected with Cape Hatteras Lighthouse since the government purchased the land from four Jennette orphans for the first lighthouse in 1803.

Rany Jennette, one of their sons, explains in an oral history that he was not isolated or deprived as a child. Several other large families lived close by, and people in the village of Buxton loved to visit the lighthouse. Rany remembers that his father made $157 a month as principal keeper. During the Depression, this was a good salary for a steady, respectable government job that provided stability for the family.

Rany was born in 1921. When he was young, he recalls, "the beach was mostly flat and undisturbed." In the 1930s, the Civilian Conservation Corps built up the dunes that now parallel the beach. Children went to school in Buxton until the eleventh grade—a twelfth school year was added statewide in the 1940s. Sometimes they would walk the two miles on sandy trails, but usually a car would pass and children could hitch a ride on the running boards. In 1933, a hurricane moved up the coast with one-hundred-mile winds and hit Hatteras Island full force. The keepers' families moved to Buxton while the three keepers stayed at their posts. Rany never returned to live at the lighthouse.

The Outer Banks have been called a "ribbon of sand." The beach may seem planted here permanently, but its shape changes all the time. Barrier islands protect the mainland from the violence of storms and ocean current. Since they're the first line of defense against wave and wind, they're constantly moving mostly in a southwesterly direction toward the mainland. Left alone, the islands might disintegrate on the ocean side but stretch out on the sound side. When the CCC built artificial dunes along the beach, it planted grasses to stabilize the soil. The high mound of sand with a thin layer of beach grass holding it together looks like a man losing his hair. Sea oats, one of the beach grasses, is on the North Carolina license plate. With its deep roots, sea oats trap blowing sand, starting the process of building a new dune. They're well suited to the ocean environment. The dunes separate the beach from NC 12. When sand overflows on the road, it's pushed back onto the beach. Now bulldozers, parked along the road, are waiting to be called to service. Almost two million people visited the National Seashore in 2011. With houses, tourist accommodations and businesses all along the coast, nature is not going to be left to its own devices.


## OFF-ROAD VEHICLES ON THE BEACH

Walking on the beach for several miles is not easy. Hikers stand out in boots, packs and hiking clothes. Tire tracks from ORVs zigzag all over the sand. Do you walk on soft, level sand; meander on a slant toward the water where the sand is firmer; or go back and forth to avoid the tracks?

Off-roaders sit in beach chairs between their vehicles and metal pipes stuck into the sand where they've placed their fishing rods. Hikers pass them, careful not to trip over their lines. Not all off-roaders are here to fish. Many sit in folding chairs, read, play cards and picnic. Others just stare, mesmerized by the waves. Young people who can't be bothered to walk the two hundred feet to the beach drive on the sand to throw a Frisbee around and sail a kite. Even with all the ORV traffic, the beach is clean.

Driving on the beach is not something you decide to do on the spur of the moment. Drivers have to buy an ORV permit from one of several visitor centers in the national seashore. Though a four-wheel drive is not required, it's highly recommended. Once they approach the sand, drivers let air out of their tires to maintain adequate traction. The softer the sand, the lower the pressure needs to be. Then they have to remember to pump up their tires to normal pressure again when they get back on the road.

Cape Hatteras National Seashore was authorized by Congress in 1937 and established in 1953 as our country's first national seashore. This was before SUVs and maybe before many people could afford a summer vacation on the beach. Later, the Park Service built ramps from the road to the beach for commercial fishermen. But ORV users and recreational fishers started driving on the beach as well.

The national seashore is now a hotbed of controversy. How should the National Park Service manage the ORVs and their owners, along with piping plovers, turtles and, eventually, MST walkers?

The national seashore publishes a yearly report on the state of the vulnerable wildlife under its care. The piping plover is a seven-inch sandy-colored shorebird with a black band across its forehead. The bird has been federally listed as endangered since 1986. North Carolina is the only state that has these plovers year-round. The nesting habits of piping plovers leave them vulnerable to almost anything else on the beach. They build small, shallow depressions in the sand to deposit three or four eggs.

In 2011, researchers found fifteen breeding pairs of piping plovers with eighteen nests, the first one on April 15. The report gives the stages for each nest, such as the number of eggs, abandoned nests and hatched eggs. The bottom line is that ten chicks fledged, down from fifteen in 2010.

In the same year, 147 sea turtle nests were found, compared to 153 nests the previous year. This is the second-highest number of nests since 2000, the first year in the report. From those nests, 6,483 turtles were calculated to have emerged. In contrast, David Stick, in *The Outer Banks of North Carolina*, reports that in the 1880s, turtles were so plentiful that a fifty-pound loggerhead sold for fifty cents.

Volunteers assist biologists by nest sitting. They try to minimize potential disturbances to the nests and turtles by watching for ghost crabs and mammalian predators, including mink, raccoon and cats. Since dunes were built, the road was constructed and other human manipulations occurred on the Outer Banks, the ocean doesn't bring new sand anymore to replenish the beach. So nesting turtles drop their eggs on eroded beaches, and volunteers may need to move the nests to higher ground. It takes about two months for turtles to hatch, and the eggs can drown before that. Once the baby turtles emerge and climb through the sand to the top of the nest, they wait until dark to crawl to the beach. Any light can confuse them because they instinctively go to the brightest horizon. With natural lighting, the water reflects moonlight and turtles find their way into the sea, but light pollution causes them to go the wrong way. Twenty years later, turtles try to go back to the beach they hatched from, but the beach will probably have changed. Sea turtle reproduction is a delicate process that can fail at any point.

Oystercatchers, also on the endangered list, have a long fire engine red beak, red eyes, black head and top and white underparts. To identify this bird, all you have to see is the long red beak. They've been designated Significantly Rare by the U.S. Fish and Wildlife Service and a Species of Special Concern in North Carolina. Twenty-three pairs nested in 2011, which produced forty-nine chicks. Of those chicks, twenty-nine fledged. In 2002, only nine had fledged. If we can define ultimate success as the number of fledged birds, things are looking up.

The Park Service has temporary closures to protect nesting birds and turtles. You can't drive at night during the summer. Sections are closed for everyone around a nesting piping plover or turtle. A buffer of one thousand meters for ORVs and three hundred meters for pedestrians is required around an unfledged chick to give these birds a chance to grow up.

In 2007, Defenders of Wildlife and National Audubon Society brought a lawsuit against the National Park Service alleging that the park management was not adequately protecting various species. The Park Service developed an ORV management plan. The next year, a consent decree was reached that provided additional protection to threatened species. Now these rules have become permanent.

But a lawsuit by the Outer Banks Preservation Association, folks who want more access by ORVs, asserts that the final rules are too restrictive. Their slogan is "Preserve and Protect, not Prohibit." They claim that people are unable to use the beaches since too many sections are closed too much of the time. The media has labeled this controversy as a fight between preservation and recreation. Visitors can swim, walk, run, fly kites, bird, fish and play ball on the beach. Shouldn't these activities be considered recreational as well?

*The Creation and Establishment of Cape Hatteras National Seashore*, an administrative history of the park, notes:

> *The legislation creating Cape Hatteras National Seashore did not specifically mention motor-vehicle use or beach-driving, and historical records from the park's establishment and early years do not indicate significant local concerns about preserving the right to drive vehicles on the beach. Quite the opposite, as documented earlier in this study, local residents and state officials sought NPS support for roads, ferries, and bridges to avoid using beaches as roadways, and in return for their support of the park, local residents demanded NPS agreement to allow commercial fishing and hunting. The law did, however, clearly specify NPS authority to regulate the beaches for uses consistent with the purposes for which the park was established.*

This issue will not be put to rest anytime soon.

You might see an oystercatcher digging in the sand. But the chance of seeing a piping plover is miniscule. Maybe if ORV activists could actually see a piping plover in its natural habitat, they would have more sympathy for the rules. Is one thousand meters the right distance for a buffer? Let the professionals in the National Park Service do their job. The rules will probably change like the beach itself.

## BUXTON, A TRAIL TOWN?

Choosing a trail town in the Outer Banks is not easy. The MST goes through several small communities, but none is large enough to stand out as an obvious candidate. Ocracoke is a great place to spend a couple of days—you could have a good time here for a couple of months—but it comes too early in the Outer Banks stretch. Food and lodging on Ocracoke are not cheap because the town is on an island accessible only by ferry.

Buxton is ten feet above sea level, which in this neck of the woods is significant. The town is tucked into the Cape Hatteras woods, giving it more protection than the other towns on the island. Conner's Supermarket, with a large selection of foods, is a good place to resupply for the rest of your hike. Seafood restaurants of every price range flourish, and the local food is superb. But don't expect too many fast-food places or all-you-can-eat restaurants. For regional literature and to learn what's going on in Hatteras Island, stop at Buxton Village Books. A couple of marinas have coin-operated laundromats, but it might be best to have done your last laundry in New Bern.

Most businesses in Buxton are located on NC 12. But in this section, the MST turns off the road and heads toward Cape Hatteras Lighthouse. So unless you need a bed, a meal or some food to put in your pack, you'll end up missing Buxton altogether.

## Salvo, Waves and *Nights in Rodanthe*

The villages of Salvo, Waves and Rodanthe offer excellent seafood restaurants, a couple of distinctive craft stores and a replica of one of the smallest post offices in the country. You can rent out every kind of water sports equipment you can think of and some you've never thought of trying—hang gliding, parasailing, wake boarding, standup paddle boarding and kite boarding. Most of these sports depend on the power of the wind to propel the rider. Just watching folks pick up the wind and fly is thrilling. Wilbur and Orville Wright chose to come to the Outer Banks to experiment with flight because of the powerful wind and soft sand to land on.

Everything here seems to be named Midgett: Midgett real estate offices, campground, gas station and convenience store. The Joseph "Mac" Midgett Water Plant was chosen the best-tasting municipal drinking water in North Carolina in 2003. Midgetts fill a cemetery along NC 12. The Midget family in the Outer Banks (with only one "t" then) can be traced to Matthew Midget, who obtained a land grant in 1722 for Bodie Island. He left several sons who were fruitful and multiplied to carry on the family name.

Rodanthe, the last town until you're out of Cape Hatteras, used to be called Chicamacomico. But maybe the name was too long, and it became Rodanthe, named after a flower from western Australia that has never seen North Carolina. The town was made famous by the movie *Nights in Rodanthe*, starring Diane Lane and Richard Gere and written by Nicholas Sparks, who lives in New Bern. Adrienne, middle-aged and divorced, is taking care of an inn for a friend. A stranger, Paul, comes to town and turns out to be the only

A replica of a tiny post office in Salvo.

guest at the inn. He also has his own demons to deal with. Together, they survive a coastal storm, but they don't go on to live happily ever after. The movie is a sweet romantic drama.

The house might be the most memorable part of the movie. After the filming, the house was moved because it was about to fall into the sea. Movie fans tried to climb the rickety stairs during frequent storms, not the safest thing to do. Saving the house became a major project for its owners after the town wanted to condemn the structure. The famous blue shutters have been replaced. The interior of the house was redone to match the movie, including the floral wallpaper and antiques. You can rent this vacation house, with its six bedrooms and four and a half baths. Alternatively, you can be like most tourists and just photograph it.

## Pea Island National Wildlife Refuge: Sustaining a Wildlife Habitat

Pea Island was once an island but no more; now it's located on the northern end of Hatteras Island. According to David Stick, an inlet, then called New Inlet, first appeared on a map in 1738 and remained more or less open until 1922. It reopened again for a short while in the hurricane of 1933, the same hurricane that forced the Cape Hatteras Lighthouse keepers out of their homes. But designations die slowly, and the refuge was named for a nonexistent island.

The thirteen miles of trail through Pea Island National Wildlife Refuge are all on the beach; there are no towns to break up the walk. The section starts at the Pea Island sign and finishes at the Bonner Bridge. In a thunderstorm, a hiker, probably carrying metal hiking poles, will be the highest thing on the beach. If the weather really deteriorates, MST hikers can run to the road.

The big difference between Pea Island and the previous beach walks is that the refuge doesn't allow driving on the beach and has no ORV ramps. There appears to be an increase in the number of birds on this beach, with more pelicans and sanderlings, whole flock of ducks and a couple of oystercatchers. You might even see a shark.

This stretch of beach is empty. Everyone would have to walk to get here, so only a few visitors venture where there's easy access to the beach. Since there are no landmarks, it's difficult to estimate progress as you walk. A blue water tower and the outline of the Bodie Island Lighthouse are somewhere out there, a long way off.

The refuge was named for beach peas, which are native throughout the eastern United States and Canada. Peas bear pale purple flowers in spring and mature on the inland side of the dunes just as migratory geese arrive in October. The purpose of the refuge is to provide a proper habitat for migratory birds and shore birds on the Atlantic flyway. Birds need a safe environment to nest, feed and rest, and the public should have a place to see birds without being expert birders.

The Visitor Center at Pea Island National Wildlife Refuge is across the road from the beach. A spotting scope is set up in front of three large windows that overlook North Pond. But what is a refuge doing in the middle of a national park?

"Pea Island Refuge was created in 1938," volunteer Ron Marchand explains. "Before that, the land was owned by several private clubs that hunted waterfowls. So we were here before Cape Hatteras National Seashore. The national seashore wasn't created until 1953." Ron staffs the visitor center desk and volunteers as a turtle watcher.

Close to the Pea Island Visitor Center, there's a walkway and lookout station, part of the Charles Kuralt Trail. The trail was named after the broadcast journalist who "shared the delights and wonders of out-of-the-way places like these."

For the general public, this area may be considered out of the way, but for MST walkers, the refuge visitor center is a landmark, an oasis on the beach walk across Pea Island. Kuralt Trails are short trails in eleven wildlife refuges in coastal Virginia and North Carolina, not one continuous trail.

The Army Corps of Engineers built impoundments to regulate the flow of water and create the best habitat for birds. It fashioned a series of dikes, sand dunes and three ponds. In the summer, mosquitoes can be fierce around the visitor center and North Pond. The refuge is well known as a birder's paradise. On the half-mile North Pond Wildlife Trail, visitors have an opportunity to see remarkable wildlife. Observation towers with free spotting scopes have been placed around the pond. Though the best birding is during the fall and winter, the refuge is managed to encourage birds all year-round. And that translates to tourist dollars. Birders are among the most affluent eco-tourists. Canoeists and kayakers, beachcombers, surf and sound anglers and nature photographers also bring money to the area, and so do MST hikers.

Continuing north on the beach, you'll reach an inlet where NC 12 used to be. In 2011, Hurricane Irene created two inlets, and one has since been filled in. The second one that some people refer to as the *new* new inlet is now bridged by a rickety metal bridge that rattles when you drive over it. Walk a few feet under the bridge to see the old cracked roadbed going into the water. The temporary bridge was constructed quickly after the hurricane, but a permanent bridge will take a lot more discussion and study. On the

Outer Banks, this new inlet is history, or maybe geology, in the making. Ocracoke Inlet is old and stable, but other inlets have opened up relatively recently, and some have closed.

The newest inlet provides another opportunity to enjoy the seashore. Visitors are kite boarding, surfing, fishing or just sitting on the sand. The ocean is rough, and waves are high; this is not a swimming beach. If you look carefully on the eastern side of the bridge, out in the waves, you can see the vertical logs that supported the foundation for the old Pea Island Lifesaving Station.

## REMEMBERING THE PEA ISLAND LIFESAVING STATION

Before the U.S. Lifesaving Service was created, volunteers would assist mariners in trouble and often take their cargo as payment. Once the service was formed, the men in charge of the station, called keepers, were first chosen based on political patronage. But after several botched rescues, Richard Etheridge, a former slave, was appointed at Pea Island in 1879. While there were mixed-race crews on the Outer Banks before, white surf men didn't want to work for an African American keeper. The Pea Island Lifesaving Station became the first and only all–African American group of surfers.

Etheridge, a former sergeant in the U.S. Colored Troops during the Civil War, ran his station in military fashion. He recorded the condition of the wind and surf, the type and number of ships sighted and details of beach patrol. When his men weren't walking their beat looking for boats in trouble, they trained. They rehearsed boat maneuvers, flags and signals and first aid. *Fire on the Beach* by David Wright and David Zoby explains, "For Etheridge and other keepers of his ilk, readiness was all."

Etheridge died on the job in 1900, but the station remained an all–African American crew. In 1915, the Lifesaving Service merged with the Revenue Cutter Service to become the United States Coast Guard. Still the Pea Island Station stayed active until 1947. Like most of these buildings, the station was in danger of falling apart. But a man who loved the outdoors and fishing bought it in the 1960s and moved it to Salvo. His grandson, Ron Pettit, and Ron's wife, Kathy, now live here with their three children and own Hatteras Watersports next door. They've updated the inside to make it livable for a growing family. A new kitchen was installed since the original site had a separate cookhouse. A dormitory originally used by the surfers was split into several bedrooms. But the outside of the building was left much the same. Still, the family plans to move to a bigger house. They're hoping to make a library out of the historic lifesaving station, if they can find adequate funding. Currently the Salvo, Waves and Rodanthe triad of communities does not have a public library.

At the northern end of Pea Island, a large house, formerly the Oregon Inlet Lifesaving Station, sits looking empty and forlorn. Its windows have been secured, the roof has new shingles and the structure has been raised on pilings to protect it from flooding. The North Carolina Aquarium owns the 1897 building, now on the National Register of Historic Places. Hopefully the station will be called to duty again, this time as an education center.

Lifesaving stations were constructed at least every seven miles in high-risk areas. On the MST route, fourteen lifesaving stations were originally in operation. How many of these buildings can reasonably be saved? Several were demolished by fire or hurricanes. Some are barely hanging on. A few buildings have been stabilized but are still empty. The rest are being used either by the National Park Service or as private residences. The buildings that have been repurposed have probably the best chance of surviving. The others remain at the mercy of the environment.


## BODIE ISLAND

Oregon Inlet and Hatteras Inlet both opened up in the September 1846 hurricane. The first vessel to pass through Oregon Inlet was named *Oregon*, and the name stuck. The MST goes over Oregon Inlet on the Herbert C. Bonner Bridge. The bridge looks like a modern steel sculpture. First it hovers low above the marsh. Then it takes off into the sky and over the shipping channel, reminiscent of Linn Cove Viaduct on Grandfather Mountain. Driving or walking over the bridge feels like you're flying on water. Before the bridge was opened in 1963, people crossed Oregon Inlet by ferry. The bridge was meant to last thirty years, and its replacement is long overdue.

After years of study and public input, the North Carolina Department of Transportation has finished its design work for a stronger new bridge and will start construction soon. It's tough to build a fixed bridge on a moving island of sand. Hopefully the new bridge will include a wider walkway for long-distance hikers. But for now, MST hikers need to cross the Bonner Bridge carefully. Others decide that it's safer to somehow get a ride across the inlet.

Bodie Island Lighthouse.

Once on Bodie Island, the trail quickly goes into the maritime forest on the Bodie Island Dike Trail. The Bodie Island Lighthouse, the northernmost lighthouse on Cape Hatteras National Seashore, is not as well visited as Cape Hatteras Lighthouse. This is the third Bodie Island Lighthouse. The first, built in 1847, literally lost its foundation. In less than ten years, the lighthouse leaned so much that the lamps were out of sync, and it was declared useless. A second lighthouse was built just before the Civil War. After the North captured the Outer Banks, retreating Confederates removed the lens and destroyed the lighthouse, leaving the area in darkness.

The current lighthouse was erected in 1872, well away from the inlet and between the ocean and the sound. It will be around a long time. But after all those years of service, the lighthouse needs almost continuous care.

The Bodie Island Lighthouse was being renovated when contractors found significant structural problems. They stopped work while the National Park Service looked for more money to complete the work. In the meantime, the scaffolding was removed. Now that more funding has been allocated, the restorations will continue. Hopefully visitors soon will be able to climb to the top again.

The lighthouse, with its black-and-white horizontal stripes, stands within an area almost untouched by modern life. A small house stands in front where fuel was stored. A double keepers' house was built for three keepers and their families. The keeper's bedroom faced the lighthouse because a keeper was always on the job. The building now houses a small visitor center.

## Jockey's Ridge State Park: A World of Sand and Wind

After a few miles of empty beach, buildings start to appear. The MST has left Cape Hatteras National Seashore. Goodbye Cape Hatteras, hello Nags Head—what a difference. As the first town outside the national seashore, Nags Head is filled with fast-food restaurants, chain motels and gift shops selling sand buckets, T-shirts and skimpy bathing suits. A long row of houses, built too close to a changing ocean, is now derelict and condemned. They're slowly being swallowed up by the sea. A yellowing condemnation sign says, "This building is condemned by building inspector. This building is unfit for human habitation. The use and occupation of this building for human habitation is prohibited and unlawful."

These houses, built on stilts, needed long, steep staircases to get to the front doors. Most houses have sandbags in front or around the stilts, but all those precautions have not worked. The quickest way to show that the houses are no longer habitable is to knock off the bottom part of the staircase. Some houses are askew, and most have their front posts in the water. Staring at those houses is both fascinating and horrifying; it's like watching a train wreck.

Smaller houses farther back on a little rise sit flat on the ground, still occupied. If the condemned houses were demolished, the second row would have a gorgeous sea view. But for now, they face large, tilting wooden megahouses.

The condemned houses serve as a reminder that the narrowing beach doesn't just affect nesting turtles. Stanley R. Riggs and his colleagues wrote in *The Battle for North Carolina's Coast*, "In its natural state, the coastal system is far from fragile. It is a high-energy, storm dependent system generally characterized by environmental extremes. Barrier islands are built by storms and are dependent on storm events to maintain their short-term health and long-term evolution. It is the fixed human structures superimposed on this dynamic system that are fragile."

Condemned houses in Nags Head.

A figure in the book shows a 2003 aerial photograph of the Avon-Buxton portion of the national seashore. The authors have drawn in where the original NC 12 was built in 1955. The road was rebuilt in 1974, 1999 and again in 2003. All the while, the island gets skinnier than a fashion model. And in the Avon-Buxton area, development is relatively modest, compared to Nags Head and north.

The name "Nags Head" could have come from several legends. Sailors might have come from Nags Head in England. Another theory is that the hills here look like a horse's head when you approach them from the sea. But the most popular story concerns pirates on the beach at night trying to lure ships to their destruction in shallow waters. They would tie a lantern to the neck of an old horse, a nag, and walk it back and forth. The up and down swinging of the light would look like another ship, and the unsuspecting sailors would steer toward it.

In Nags Head, the trail passes two fishing piers. Men and young boys have a line out and just sit and stare at the surf. The kids seem awfully bored. There are no off-road vehicles on this city beach. The trail continues on NC 12, here called Beach Road, a city street. You cross U.S. 158, the bypass road with fast-food restaurants and beach stores, and see people hang gliding off the dunes. The Wright Brothers National Memorial is only a couple of miles north. Wilbur and Orville Wright came from Ohio to experiment with human-powered flight. The winds were right for flying, the sand was soft for landing and the locals were very cooperative.

A small Mountains-to-Sea Trail sign stands at the entrance to Jockey's Ridge State Park. Since almost all visitors drive into the park, no one will notice the sign or the trail. Though Jockey's Ridge State Park is a small state park, about 420 acres, it is the most visited state park in North Carolina, with over 1.3 million people in 2011. The park has the tallest natural sand dune in the East. The end of the trail is not at sea level, as Mountains-to-*Sea* might imply, but rather at ninety to one hundred feet, depending on the shifting sand.

Though small, the park has several ecological systems. The area around the visitor center is in a maritime forest with live oaks, wax myrtle and red cedar. Along the Roanoke Sound Estuary, cattails and saw grass provide a home for waterfowl and fish. Blue herons and snowy egrets frequent the sound. But it's the sand dunes on top that are breathtaking.

The park makes good use of the wind. Close to the visitor center, a wind turbine creates enough energy to power the building. The turbine, the first in a North Carolina state park, stands about seventy feet high, with a propeller diameter of twenty-three feet.

Each state park has a different history. Some are the result of a large number of volunteers. For other parks, one person gets the credit for protecting the land for public use. Carolista Baum will always be remembered as the woman who stood in front of bulldozers in 1973 after the land was sold for development. She vowed to preserve the dunes and found the right political climate to organize people and lobby the state legislature to save Jockey's Ridge.

Are you ready for the finale? The last climb starts on a boardwalk where most visitors congregate. They look at the interpretive signs and argue within their group about whether to stop here or continue on the sand. You'll walk up to the sand dunes, the biggest climb since Hanging Rock State Park, miles and weeks back. The soft sand makes the trail feel surprisingly steep, two steps forward and one step back. Wind and sand are blowing hard, so watch out for your hat.

The top of the dune looks like the Sahara Desert. Technically, the ridge is an example of a medano, defined as a huge hill of shifting sand without vegetation. Roanoke Sound is on one side and the Atlantic Ocean on the other. Though it's only one hundred feet above sea level, it feels like the top of the world.

Because the high point is just bare sand, the elevation varies with the changing wind. Alternating airflows concentrate the sand at the crest of the dune and keep the sand from blowing away. For children and for adults as well, this might be the biggest sandbox in the world. It's ideal for flying a kite. You can learn to hang glide here. After a period of heavy rain, pools of fresh water stand in the low spots between the dunes.

The finish line is on the highest dune the day you complete the trail. You've been following the white circles and directions on the road for weeks, but now you're free to take your own path up to the finish line. Don't expect to find an MST sign at the top. A sign would blow away, and besides, the end point changes with the wind at the moment.

You're at the end of your MST adventure. After taking picture after picture of the sand, the ocean and Roanoke Sound, and having your picture taken, you'll slide down the sand, feeling victorious. But there's one more step. If you've just completed the MST here, you should stop by the park visitor center, introduce yourself to the staff and sign the visitor book. Superintendent Debo Cox will be so happy to see you and make a fuss. He'll shower you with congratulations and take your picture, which will go on the MST bulletin board.

Superintendent Cox feels a passion for the trail. He writes:

> *The Mountains-to-Sea Trail represents the best of what North Carolina has to offer. People have a chance to embark on an adventure that will take them through some of the state's most beautiful and treasured places. As the eastern terminus of the trail we've had a chance to talk to some amazing travelers who've made the journey. It's a journey not only of miles, but of personal experience as well. All that's required is that they take the first step. One of the highlights of hikers who've completed the trip is coming in to the Jockey's Ridge Visitor Center and reading the comments of others who've literally walked in their footsteps. That shared personal experience is what makes the MST bigger than just a winding path between two points. It becomes an adventure that takes on a life of its own.*

Whether you're on a day hike or plan to walk a thousand miles, you'll love the Mountains-to-Sea Trail. So get out there.

## ON REACHING THE END OF THE TRAIL

Walking the MST fulfilled my primary mission to see and understand my state. Now, no matter what I sound like, I'm a North Carolinian. Whenever I met someone on the trail, I asked, "Hey, do you know you're on the MST?" Several times while walking the road, drivers would stop to point in a general western direction and say, "Lady, the A.T. is that way." Yes, but I'm on MST, buddy.

As Sharon McCarthy says when she speaks to groups in Western North Carolina, "You need to get out of the mountains, folks." I'm in the mountains all the time—that's practically my day job now. What remains with me is not so much the pristine woods and wilderness but the farms and open areas in the mountains east of Blowing Rock. I was intrigued by the clever way the trail entered and left the state parks in the Piedmont. I loved the thrill and almost naughty feeling of walking on private land and hope more landowners allow hikers on their property.

I discovered a new world of tobacco, cotton and small churches that I never would have seen whizzing by in a car. Though this is also North Carolina, it was a foreign land to me. I read the names on the graves in the roadside cemetery, the same family names over and over again. Tromping on the beach, I sang, "This land is your land."

But most important, I'll remember all the new friends I made as a result of hiking the trail—the people who walked with me, gave me rides and let me stay at their houses, even though I had never met them before. Ultimately, for me, the MST is about the people who walk, maintain and care about the trail.

# Chapter 6
# The MST's Past and Future

An entire book can be written about the history of the MST and probably will be. You can trace the genesis of the MST back to 1968, when Congress passed the National Trails Systems Act to encourage outdoor recreation. In 1973, the North Carolina General Assembly passed its version, the North Carolina Trails Systems Act, "in order to provide for the ever-increasing outdoor recreation needs of an expanded population." At the time, there was no initial suggestion for a foot trail that would span the state. A Trails Committee was created to advise the state on issues dealing with trails. This committee is still active today.

Jim Hallsey, who became trails coordinator for the State Parks System, first plotted the route on paper. His plan was accepted by the Trails Committee. On September 9, 1977, at the Fourth National Trails Symposium at Lake Junaluska outside of Waynesville, Howard Lee, then secretary of the North Carolina Department of Natural Resources and Community Development, announced the idea of a long-distance trail for North Carolina.

"I want our State Trails Committee to look at recommending a trail that would give North Carolinians and national visitors using it a real feel for the sights, sounds and people of the state," Howard Lee said to the almost four hundred conference participants. Lee, a lifelong educator and legislator, may have seemed like an unlikely advocate for a trail through North Carolina, but when the opportunity presented itself, he championed the Mountains-to-Sea Trail. In his book, *The Courage to Lead*, Howard Lee calls the start, announcement and initiation of the MST one of his proudest achievements.

In a recent interview, Lee recalled, "The MST wasn't my idea. I didn't know much about trails." Lee's speechwriter asked, "Can I put in something that you'll commit yourself to a trail across the state?" Lee called Governor Jim Hunt to clear it with him. As he recalls, "Hunt said, 'Don't commit any money.'" At the time, they thought that the trail would be about 450 miles long.

A cooperative agreement was signed between the state, National Park Service, U.S. Fish and Wildlife Service and the U.S. Forest Service to kick-start the construction of the trail by volunteer groups. In 1982, a 75.8-mile trail along the Cape Hatteras National Seashore became the first segment of the trail to be designated part of the MST. Hallsey remembers that the ceremony was in the shadow of the Cape Hatteras Lighthouse. Hallsey and his colleagues had installed MST logo signs at major access points, knowing that they probably wouldn't last long in the salt-air environment. One of those signs, weathered and faded, is still standing at a trailhead near the lighthouse's new location.

Allen de Hart, who wrote *Hiking North Carolina's Mountains-to-Sea Trail*, was one of the first two people to finish the MST in 1997. De Hart, a retired college professor, is considered the grandfather of the MST. He was involved in the planning for the MST from the beginning. When interest for the trail seemed to wane, Allen, with his former students, started Friends of the MST in 1997.

The State of North Carolina worked out the trail route from segments already available on public land, but Allen designed the road sections, taken mostly from bicycle routes. The trail became part of the North Carolina State Park System in 2000. The road segments of the MST, however, are not officially part of the state park.

The history of the trail is very recent. Most people involved in the creation of and propelling the trail forward are still alive and active today. Recently several MST leaders speculated on what the MST will be like in 2027, the fiftieth anniversary of the trail.

## JEFF BREWER, FIRST PRESIDENT OF FRIENDS OF THE MST

In 2027, the MST will be completed on trails and greenways from Clingmans Dome to Smithfield in the Coastal Plains. The East will be our major area of work and will slowly come together. The ultimate challenge is how to get the MST from Smithfield to Jockey's Ridge in the Outer Banks. We will have campsites on the Blue Ridge Parkway and others areas in central North Carolina. I often wonder how stable the trail will be on the Outer Banks, due to hurricanes and the rise in sea level.

I can also see major trail connections that will unite the MST to the A.T. One connection could be from the Boone and Blowing Rock area to Roan Mountain. Another from Doughton Park could follow the parkway up to connect to the A.T at Peaks of Otter in Virginia. These would create very long loops and figure eights in the mountain region.

I can also see that Friends of the MST will become so strong with volunteers and staff that the ultimate responsibility of the MST would be moved away from the Division of Parks and Recreation and placed in the hands of the FMST by the North Carolina state legislature. North Carolina volunteers will continue to be the driving force and make the MST into the flagship trail that was envisioned back in 1977.


## Allen de Hart, Granddaddy of the MST

I believe the MST end points (Clingmans Dome and Jockey's Ridge) will remain the same. I don't think the state would rescind its earlier designations. I believe the Friends of the MST as an organization will survive and be the leading nonprofit organization for planning, guidance and influence.

The FMST bylaws has for its mission a hiking route only, but I predict the trail will continue to be used for hiking, bicycling, horseback riding and canoeing. When the trail turns fifty years old, hikers will still walk pieces on state and county bicycling routes. A canoeing alternate route will include a section of the Neuse River. I think there will be little motivation to change the currently constructed and designated parkway routing. Neither will there be changes in the routing planned along the Haw River, Eno River and Neuse River. Any changes on Cape Hatteras would be minor.

Trail culture will continue to increase among cities and towns. For example, options in the Triad and connecting loops in the Durham/Raleigh area will provide the highest number of users. Continued growth of campsite options will increase the number of long-distance hikers. The state will eventually approve campsites for those who are rafting.

I believe that the impact on North Carolina would be outstanding because it would be the state with the second-longest state trail, after the Florida

Scenic Trail, east of the Mississippi. There will be new guidebooks for route usage, some on specific areas such as mountains only, the Triad, the Triangle or the coast.

In fifty years, there is likely to be a book on all or some of those who have completed the MST—hiking alone, with others, the oldest, the youngest, the runners and those on special missions such as flora, fauna or historic sites.

## KATE DIXON,
## EXECUTIVE DIRECTOR OF FRIENDS OF THE MST

By 2027, I predict that the Mountains-to-Sea Trail will be one of the biggest tourist attractions in North Carolina. It will be used and loved by people who live near it. MST trail towns will work to promote the trail in their area and help to make hiking the MST a great experience.

Hundreds of thousands of people will enjoy the trail each year. The vast majority of these people will be day-hikers, out to explore a new area or to revisit one that they love. But I expect that the numbers of people completing the entire MST will skyrocket from where it is now. Many MST completers will be section hikers who hike the trail over several years as a way to learn more about North Carolina. Others will immerse themselves in the trail and the physical and mental challenge of a thru-hike.

Despite changes, I expect that the experience of hiking the trail will be fundamentally the same in 2027 as it is today. All hikers will have moments, grand and small, when the beauty of North Carolina takes their breath away. The trail will challenge them in personal ways that are new and meaningful. And finally, they will meet people who help them become new friends and show them the best of North Carolina.

## JIM HALLSEY,
## RETIRED NORTH CAROLINA STATE PARK CHIEF RANGER

The MST will continue to be North Carolina's premier cross-state trail among an expanding statewide network of regional, interconnected long-distance, multi-modal trails. While no one can reliably predict when a hiking trail across the state will be completed, the principles of multiple use trails will prevail in locating, designing and building the present "missing links" of the MST. As originally envisioned, the MST will continue to connect the state's outstanding natural resources, historic and cultural features with an ever-growing and more urban population in search of remote and wild places for outdoor recreation.

The types of trail users and modes of trail travel on the MST will be more diverse than those of today, including increased numbers of seniors and youth and more water trail, bike trail and equestrian trail segments. Consequently, there will be new opportunities for local support groups, facilities and information that promote a much broader spectrum of the population experiencing portions of the MST. While a few hearty individuals with ample leisure will continue to thru-hike or section-hike the entire trail, they will constitute a small and diminishing proportion of total MST users.

## DANNY BERNSTEIN

The trail will change, due to regional and even national involvement. We need to remember that so much of the trail is on federal land. People will come from all over the eastern United States and beyond to hike the whole trail. It's happened already. Scot Ward came from Kentucky to hike the trail four times. William Dolling, the first international completer, made several trips from Cumbria in northern England to walk the trail in sections. So the MST is not just for North Carolinians. If the MST connects with the A.T., as Jeff Brewer speculates, many hikers will do a loop or a diversion off the MST. Some of the trail will always be on roads. I hope that the MST will never all be on a footpath between two sets of trees.

Almost everyone who walks across the state now keeps a blog filled with pictures on their progress. By 2027, hikers will publish books on their trail experience. The trail will have an official MST guidebook, which will be revised regularly. Whether hikers follow the white circles for a few miles off the Blue Ridge Parkway, see the MST map on a sign in Eno River State Park or Open Pond Trail on the Outer Banks, they'll know that they're walking on the Mountains-to-Sea Trail.

## Chapter 7

# What People Want to Know about Walking the MST

*What map or guidebook did you follow?*

The MST footpath is marked with white circles. I also carried National Geographic maps for the mountain section. Once on the road, I used Scot Ward's *The Thru-Hiker's Manual for the Mountains-to-Sea Trail of North Carolina*, published in 2012. It's a self-published booklet in spreadsheet form.

*How long did it take you to walk the trail?*

It took me seventy-eight hiking days for 985 miles with almost 100,000 feet of ascent. Your mileage will vary, depending on the trail route at the time you're walking it. You can also ride a bike on the road sections of the MST.

*How far did you walk each day?*

The average was about twelve and a half miles a day. That's low because it included lots of half days as I finished a section and went home. On mountain trails, ten to twelve miles is a reasonable average. Once out of the mountains, you can do fifteen miles or more. It might be difficult for mountain hikers to understand that you can walk fifteen miles or more day after day.

*Where did you camp?*

There are few legal places to camp. I backpacked in the Smokies and in Croatan National Forest. I could have backpacked through Linville Gorge and Wilson Creek. You can't camp on Blue Ridge Parkway land. Some hikers camp in Nantahala and Pisgah Forest, just off the parkway.

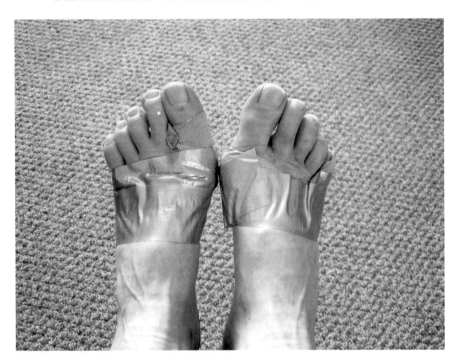

Walking the beach is hard on your feet.

*Then where did you stay?*

That was part of the challenge. For some of the mountain section, I stayed in my house in Asheville. After that, I stayed in people's houses, in campgrounds and in inns and motels, depending on the section I was hiking.

*But what about your car?*

That was another part of the challenge. My hiking partner, Sharon, and I each took our cars, which we put on either end of the trail for the day. When we reached our destination, we drove back to pick up the car at the beginning of the trail. When I walked a section by myself, I hired shuttlers, who helped me place my car at the end of the section for the day. They dropped me off at the beginning, and I then walked to my car.

*What is a car shuttle?*

Here's how it works:

On the first day, drive two cars where you'll end your hike tonight and leave car A. With car B, drive back to the beginning of the trail. Leave car B here and hike. At the end of the day, you're at car A. Drive back to the beginning of the hike to pick up car B. Take both cars, drive to your end point for the next day and leave car A there. Go to your lodging for the night with car B. The next day, drive car B to the beginning and walk to car A.

Repeat the process. It is much more complicated to write out than to do it.

*What were the highlights for you?*
The Smokies.
Moses Cone and Doughton Parks on the Blue Ridge Parkway.
Walking twenty-five miles of new trail on the Blue Ridge Parkway just after it opened. I went to the official opening and dedication of this section and then hiked through it the next week.
Great places to visit—Sylva, Freeborne Motel in Laurel Springs, Glencoe Mill Village and Emily's Cookies north of Burlington, New Bern and Ocracoke.
Meeting people on the road. People were friendly, curious, puzzled and always trying to be helpful.

*If there were highlights, there must have been lowlights.*
Loose dogs. I don't have to think twice about that. In many rural areas, dogs are not fenced or leashed. As I passed a house, a dog started barking and ran after me. It then excited the dog in the next house, and pretty soon I might have a pack of dogs encircling me. I carried pepper spray, though I never had to use it.

*Wasn't it dangerous on the road?*
The road sections of the MST are on back roads, usually NC bicycle routes. I wasn't walking on interstate highways. I waved to every car that went by, not an Appalachian one-finger wave or a limp wave like the queen mother. My wave was hard and energetic.
I wore an orange vest for visibility and watched for cars on blind curves. I felt that road angels were watching out for me on back roads: police officers, letter carriers, UPS and FedEx drivers and others in company vehicles. I waved extra hard at them.

*Will MST hikers have trail names?*
Probably, but only when there are enough people on the trail. Usually another hiker gives you a trail name, based on something you said or did. On the A.T., my husband, Lenny, and I stuck with our first names. "Danny and Lenny" already sounded like a comedy team.

*When is the best time to do the MST?*

If you're doing it in sections, you can pick the best time for each part. However, if you're looking to walk the trail in one shot—I hesitate to call it a thru-hike—you can consider several time frames, each with advantages and disadvantages.

**Spring hike:** Start at Clingmans Dome at the beginning of April. Clingmans Dome Road opens April 1, if the weather cooperates. It will be cold on top, but you'll be off the mountain very quickly. You'll have spring flowers in the mountains and cool weather. You'll end up on the coast at the beginning of June, enjoying long days before the summer crowds arrive.

**Fall hike:** Start at Clingmans Dome in early September, and you'll be walking through autumn colors at the higher altitudes. There will be plenty of fall flowers, and it will still be warm. You'll need to know what the rules and recommendations are in hunting season for each national forest and refuge and on the Sauratown Trail. When you get to the Outer Banks in early November, most of the bugs and tourists will be gone. Some visitor services will be closed, but fall bird migration will be in full swing.

**Summer hike:** You'll enjoy long warm days and summer flowers. There will be more day hikers on the trail. All the tourist services will be open. No matter when you do it, you'll love it.

# Bibliography

M ost of the material comes from actually walking the Mountains-to-Sea Trail. The following books and websites were consulted.

Barefoot, Daniel W. *Touring North Carolina's Revolutionary War Site*. Winston-Salem, NC: John F. Blair, 1998.

Binkley, Cameron. "The Creation and Establishment of Cape Hatteras National Seashore: The Great Depression through Mission 66." National Park Service, August 2007. www.nps.gov/history/history/online_books/caha/caha_ah.pdf.

Blevins, David, and Michael P. Schafale. *Wild North Carolina*. Chapel Hill: University of North Carolina Press, 2011.

Boyette, Patsy M. "La Grange—The Garden Spot Continues to Bloom." *Olde Kinston Gazette*, September 1998.

Cape Hatteras National Seashore Resource Reports and Publications. http://www.nps.gov/caha/naturescience/protected-species-2011-annual-reports.htm.

Carr, Dawson. *Cape Hatteras Lighthouse: Sentinel of the Shoals*. Chapel Hill: University of North Carolina Press, 2000.

Clairborne, Jack, and William Price. *Discovering North Carolina: A Tar Heel Reader*. Chapel Hill: University of North Carolina Press, 1991.

DeBlieu, Jan. *Hatteras Journal*. Winston-Salem, NC: John F. Blair, 1998.

De Hart, Allen. *Hiking North Carolina's Mountains-to-Sea Trail*. Chapel Hill: University of North Carolina Press, 2000.

Ellis, Edward Barnes, Jr. *In This Small Place*. New Bern, NC: McBryde Publishing, 2005.

————. *New Bern History 101*. New Bern, NC: McBryde Publishing, 2009.

Ellis, Jerry. *Walking the Trail: One Man's Journey Along the Cherokee Trail of Tears*. Lincoln, NE: Bison Books, 2001.

Hall, Jacquelyn Dowd, James L. Leloudis, Robert Rodgers Korstag, Mary Murphy, LuAnn Jones and Christopher B. Daly. *Like a Family: The Making of a Southern Cotton Mill World*. Chapel Hill: University of North Carolina Press, 1987.

Jenette, Rany. "Cape Hatteras Lighthouse As I Knew It." http://www.nps.gov/caha/historyculture/upload/RANY's%20oral%20history%20edited%2011202008.pdf.

Kephart, Horace. *Camping and Woodcraft*. With an introduction by George Ellison. Gatlinburg, TN: Great Smoky Mountains Association, 2011.

————. *Our Southern Highlanders*. With an introduction by George Ellison. Knoxville: University of Tennessee, 1976.

Lassiter, Thomas J. "A Short History of Johnston County: 1746–1890." In *The Heritage of Johnston County North Carolina*. Winston-Salem, NC: Heritage of Johnston County Book Committee in cooperation with the History Division, Hunter Publishing Co., 1985.

Lawson, John. *A New Voyage to Carolina*. Chapel Hill: University of North Carolina Press, 1984. Originally published 1709 in London.

Lee, Howard N. *The Courage to Lead.* Chapel Hill: Cotton Patch Press, 2008.

Logue, Victoria, Frank Logue and Nicole Blouin. *Guide to the Blue Ridge Parkway.* Birmingham, AL: Menasha Ridge Press, 2003.

Mobley, Joe A. *The Way We Lived in North Carolina.* Chapel Hill: University of North Carolina Press, 2003.

New, Elisa. *Jacob's Cane. A Jewish Family's Journey from the Four Lands of Lithuania to the Ports of London and Baltimore.* New York: Basic Books, 2009.

Noblitt, Phil. *A Mansion in the Mountains.* Charlotte, NC: Catawba Publishing Company, 1996.

Phillips, Billie W. *Growing Up in Glencoe.* Self-published, n.d.

Powell, William S. *North Carolina, a History.* Chapel Hill: University of North Carolina Press, 1988.

Ready, Milton. *The Tar Heel State: A History of North Carolina.* Columbia: University of South Carolina Press, 2005.

Riggs, Stanley R., Dorothea V. Ames, Stephen J. Culver and David J. Mallinson. *The Battle for North Carolina's Coast.* Chapel Hill: University of North Carolina Press, 2011.

Shelton-Roberts, Cheryl, and Bruce Roberts. *North Carolina Lighthouses: Stories of History and Hope.* Guildford, CT: Globe Pequot Press, 2011.

Steddum, Janet. *The Battle for Falls Lake.* Raleigh, NC: Lulu Press, 2007.

Stick, David. *The Outer Banks of North Carolina.* Chapel Hill: University of North Carolina Press, 1958.

———. *An Outer Banks Reader.* Chapel Hill: University of North Carolina Press, 1998.

Tryon Palace Commission. *Tryon Palace: Its Restoration and Preservation, 1945–1965.* Self-published, n.d.

Ward, Scot. *The Thru-Hiker's Manual for the Mountains-to-Sea Trail of North Carolina, East-Bound.* Available at www.thru-hiker.us.

Weber, Walt. *Trail Profiles and Maps from the Great Smokies to Mount Mitchell and Beyond.* Asheville, NC: Grateful Steps, 2009.

West, John Foster. *The Ballad of Tom Dula: The Documented Story Behind the Murder of Laura Foster and the Trials and Execution of Tom Dula.* Boone, NC: Parkway Publishers, 2002.

Woods, Mark. *Federal Wilderness Preservation in the United States.* In *The Great New Wilderness Debate,* edited by J. Baird Callicott and Michael P. Nelson. Athens: University of Georgia Press, 1998.

Wright, David, and David Zoby. *Fire on the Beach.* New York: Scribner, 2000.

Yafa, Stephen. *Big Cotton: How a Humble Fiber Created Fortunes, Wrecked Civilizations, and Put America on the Map.* New York: Viking, 2005.

Yeargin, Billy. *North Carolina Tobacco.* Charleston, SC: The History Press, 2008.

# WEBSITES

**Blue Ridge Parkway** www.nps.gov/blri
**Cape Hatteras National Seashore** www.nps.gov/caha
**Cedar Island National Wildlife Refuge** www.fws.gov/cedarisland
**Friends of the Mountains-to-Sea Trail** www.ncmst.org
**Great Smoky Mountains National Park** www.nps.gov/grsm
In Great Smoky Mountains National Park, camping is allowed at permissible campsites with a backcountry permit. Campers need to contact the Smokies backcountry office for permit and reservation information. It's an easy, friendly process—they really do want you to get out in the backcountry.
**National Forests in North Carolina** www.fs.usda.gov/recarea/nfsnc
**North Carolina State Parks** www.ncparks.gov
**Pea Island National Wildlife Refuge** www.fws.gov/peaisland

# Index

# About the Author

Danny Bernstein's mission is to get people out of their cars and hiking. She's been a committed hiker for over forty years, completing the Appalachian Trail, all the trails in Great Smoky Mountains National Park, the South Beyond 6000 (all the mountains higher than six thousand feet in the East), many other hiking challenges and, of course, the Mountains-to-Sea Trail. Danny and her husband maintain a section of the Mountains-to-Sea Trail and a section of the Appalachian Trail on the Tennessee/North Carolina border. Trails don't maintain themselves, and people have to get out there to clip, clean and remove blow downs.

*Courtesy of Sharon McCarthy.*

Danny keeps hiking and leads hikes for the Carolina Mountain Club and Friends of the Smokies. She's on the board of directors of the Great Smoky

Mountains Association. She's written two hiking guides, *Hiking the Carolina Mountains* (2007) and *Hiking North Carolina's Blue Ridge Mountains* (2009). She blogs at www.hikertohiker.com.

In her previous life, she worked in computer science for thirty-five years, way before computing was cool, first as a software developer and then as a professor of computer science.

Her motto is "No place is too far to walk if you have the time." Danny plans to die with her boots on.

Visit us at
www.historypress.net